Inflamed
by Love

meditations
for spiritual pilgrims

Jean Fox

Madonna House Publications
2888 Dafoe Rd
Combermere ON K0J 1L0

www.madonnahouse.org/publications

First Edition

First printing, Feb. 11, 2002 — feast of Our Lady of Lourdes

Printed in Canada

Compiled by Richard Payne and edited by Richard Payne, Martin Nagy, Linda Lambeth and Marian Heiberger

Scripture quotations are taken from the New Jerusalem Bible, copyright © 1985 by Darton, Longman & Todd, London, and Doubleday, a division of Random House, Inc., New York.

National Library of Canada Cataloguing in Publication Data

Fox, Jean, 1931–
    Inflamed by love : meditations for spiritual pilgrims

ISBN 0-921440-78-2

    1. Meditations. 2. Spiritual life—Catholic authors. I. Title.

BX2350.F69 2002   242   C2002-900952-9

Design by Rob Huston

This book is set in Berkeley Oldstyle, designed by Frederic W. Goudy for the University of California Press in 1938. Heading and display text is set in Balzano, designed by America's famous carver of inscriptions, John Benson.

God is raising up an army of little souls who have become
living flames of his love—spreading love in the darkest corners of the earth.
They are making way for an entirely new "Civilization of Love."
May you be one of them.

Contents

Foreword

Near the end of her classic bestseller, *Poustinia*, Catherine Doherty wrote these words:

"The world knows about God. Because it only knows about Him, it can reject Him, ignore Him, be indifferent to Him, re-crucify Him a thousand times a day. But if the world knew Him through His own revelation of Himself to us in the poustinia of our heart, then He would not be able to be rejected. Then love would enter the world through us. We could speak His word to the world, if we lived in the poustinia of our hearts."

Although tens of thousands of Catholics, other Christians, and even non-Christians have responded to these words with a great desire to meet Christ at this core of their being that Catherine calls "poustinia of the heart," these words were originally directed to the laymen, women, and priests of Madonna House. Our Russian foundress was giving us a new and deeper vision of what it means to be a disciple and an apostle of Christ.

Through His mandate to Catherine, we had already heard and accepted His call to "preach the Gospel with our life without compromise," but in her presentation of the poustinia of the heart, Catherine was telling us that it wasn't enough to speak the Gospel with all our words and deeds. Christ wanted us to meet Him, through faith and the action of the Holy Spirit, so deeply that with Him we would become the Gospel. Then neither we nor our "hearers" could really reject Him.

For 50 years, Catherine spoke constantly of this journey inward to meet the Lord. Spoke of it? She wrote about it, exhorted us and everyone else to embark on it, dramatized it in dozens of ways, and, above all, showed us what it meant in her own daily life. For Catherine to pilgrim into the poustinia of her heart meant simultaneously to pilgrim into the heart of everyone she met, where the same Christ awaited her. Therefore it was absolutely clear to her—truly the fact above all other facts—that there was no separation between "spiritual" and "everyday" life, none at all. Every task, every duty, every person, every circumstance was an encounter with Christ. Cooking, farming, laundry, bookkeeping, car repair, writing poetry or a thank-you note, speaking and listening, swimming, eating, sorting donations, kneeling in prayer, study, brain surgery, changing a diaper—every human action was meant to be and in fact was for her a meeting with the One who, in St. Paul's words, "is everything and is in everything."[1]

It is rare to meet a Christian who truly grasps the full implication of Christ's incarnation, passion, death, descent to the dead, resurrection, ascension, enthronement, and sending of the Holy Spirit. Many of those who do grasp this "paschal Mystery" can live it out. Fewer can teach it convincingly, and fewer still can teach others to live it and teach it! By God's grace, Catherine Doherty had this gift, which entails the willingness to become truly an icon of Christ, especially in His embrace of the cross out of perfect love, so that another can see how to make the same choice in the power of the Spirit. Thus, when Jean Fox was elected director general of the women of Madonna House after Catherine died, her mission was not so impossible as it seemed. She did not have to try to fill the shoes of the foundress. Jean simply had to live

1. Colossians 3:20

what God had taught her through Catherine. This might not sound so simple, but when a holy Russian has taught you the breadth and length, the height and depth of God's mercy and the joy of the cross, it becomes possible.

Nevertheless this "it"—the totality of the Gospel life—is huge. Working closely with Jean for seven years before Catherine died and for sixteen years since, I can attest to the great generosity and prayerfulness with which Jean has lived this totality, attentive as Catherine taught her both to the vision of the whole and the minute details of community life and each individual life in her care.

In Christ's Church, as He clearly told us, leadership means service, loving and very humble service. In practice this translates into focusing on God and people, with the result that the leader who is led by the Holy Spirit will know that her or his necessary attention to structure and organization is *for the sake* of God's glory and the well-being of His people.

Some years ago, a friend and reader of *Restoration*, the monthly Madonna House newspaper, took me to task for not "letting" Jean write more than her usual "begging column," *One Man's Scrap, Another Man's Gold*. I assured my friend that no one was likely to muzzle Jean Fox and that when she was ready to write, she would. A couple of years later Jean's call to teach the daily practicalities of Gospel life in Madonna House began to find expression in frequent staff letters, brief selections of which make up the pages of *Inflamed by Love*.

As you read through these selections, you will quickly see why we at Madonna House wanted to put them into your hands. Pushed by the Holy Spirit and the dozens of new vocations He inspired after Catherine's death, Jean realized that the whole range of Madonna House life, from its Marian character to the centrality of the Liturgy to the love for poverty and prayer to connecting every single thing to Christ, needed to be explained and re-explained. Those of us formed in our apostolate by Catherine also understood that, now that she had gone home to the Lord, we needed to plunge into our life more deeply and take far greater responsibility for living it and passing it on. Jean's letters are a most significant part of the deepening of our communal growth. They make Catherine's Spirit-given understanding of all life as communion in Christ available to everyone.

As you read, you will see how Catherine could hear the line from our Little Mandate—"Listen to the Spirit. He will lead you"—as a summary of our post-Vatican II struggle to hear and obey the Holy Spirit as He works out the *divine plan* for the renewal of the Church. If Christ is everything and in everything, then He is ceaselessly breathing out the Holy Spirit to enlighten, guide, and strengthen each of us in all aspects of life so that every moment can become a "sacrament" of His presence.

You will also see in these selections from Jean's letters something of the unique way Madonna House was working over the past sixteen years to follow Pope John Paul II into the third millennium of Christ's Incarnation. It is as certain as the resurrection of His Son that God wants to give the Church and the human race a new Springtime of faith and evangelization. On our part, we will need to hold the treasure of the faith handed down to us for 2000 years with ever holier, wiser, more loving minds and hearts. We are called to plant it among peoples who have never been able to receive it and to replant it among other peoples who once received it but have now forgotten what it means. Similarly, Jean's words remind us to welcome, not fear, the One who proclaims, "Behold! I make all things new."[2]

2. Revelation 21:5

In one of her letters, Jean comments, "Who will bring forth this new creation in us? Call upon the Holy Spirit with verve and confidence. Allow the Holy Spirit to penetrate, to reveal all the untruths in your mind and heart. Step by step take your maladies. . . to the Mother of God, and she will gently and quietly give you the security and safety that you so desire. . . The restoration of this poor world will take many years, for grace builds on nature. We must allow heaven's love to penetrate us and form us into a new creation. We cannot make this happen. We must follow the Mother of God, and like her let it be done to us according to His Word."

May the stream of loving wisdom that flowed from the Holy Trinity through the heart of Our Lady of Combermere into the heart of Catherine to create and sustain Madonna House, the same stream that is flowing in these words from Jean Fox, bring you every blessing from the heart of Him who is Wisdom.

Father Robert D. Pelton
Director General of the Priests of Madonna House
Feast of the Epiphany 2002

Introduction

A page of history turned on September 11th, 2001. Another era began, the outline of which is still dim. Our hope for the future rests secure in Jesus Christ. This time of great uncertainty has brought us to a state of deep humility, simplicity, hope, and gratitude.

Great distress has ushered in this new era. Our world suffers from families torn asunder, wars and threats of wars, the dread of bombs and planes falling from the sky, and the terror of fatal microorganisms attacking us when we simply breathe and drink. What a relief it is to be wrapped in the silence and the presence of the Mother of God. She is eternally with her children, soothing us and holding us, whispering words of consolation and tenderness to us. She is there when we falter on our journey to stay faithful to her Son.

In the 1930s, several authors, including Maritain, Guardini, Sorokin, Watts, Belloc, and Berdyaev, independently came to similar conclusions, leaving behind a literary genre dubbed "crisis literature." This diverse body of thinkers surmised that we've arrived at the end of a historical era and that the transition into the next era will be catastrophic.

Some seventy years later, we're struggling through the heart of this transition. Confusion and self-interest lie at the heart of this crisis. Intellectuals, economists, politicians, and leaders of nations have built another Tower of Babel. People cannot hear or understand one another. From the furnace of this terrible confusion mankind will rise to a deeper spirituality. The Holy Father calls this flowering that will take place "the Civilization of Love."

Catherine Doherty warned us of this time. As she prepared us, her direction was clear and simple, "We must take the words of Scripture and put them into practice. Hearing the Word of God without doing it will get us nowhere."

The Holy Spirit gave Catherine and therefore us a way of putting the Word of God into practice—The Little Mandate. As we incarnate it, we will understand that the only response we can have to this world catastrophe is to let the Little Mandate sing in our heart. Pray every day for the fire of God's love to ignite your heart. Pray every day for the gift of faith. Pray every day that God's will be done on earth as it is in heaven.

The twentieth century yielded the Church more martyrs than all other centuries of Christianity. The blood of the martyrs is the seed of faith. We can with great hope and profound faith be assured there will be a dramatic blossoming of Christianity, the like of which the earth has never seen. With the Holy Father leading us, we are assured that Our Lady and her Son, and all of heaven, will grace us as never before. Ask for whatever you need. Do so with childlike confidence. Signs of a springtime in the Church bloom in every corner. Love's transforming power will come to you wherever you are. Just let God do with you what he will. Our work is to say "Yes" and to resound a fervent "Thank You" for everything that happens each day, the rest God will do.

Our purification is underway. We've been on the cross for some time. Fear nothing! The power of God's mercy is rushing through our bodies and minds, hearts and souls. It will do so with increasing vehemence in the days ahead. Expect miracles. Expect new life. Expect a surge in the joy and love of the cross. Each of us has been called to personally stand

with firmness and resolve. We are being called to do so collectively, as well. Hold one another in prayer as human
beings, so that God's love will wash through us as Christ's
body with greater intensity than we can hope or imagine.

We must believe as we have never believed before in the
history of Christianity. Our days in this time, as a page turns
in history, must be filled with the knowledge and awareness
that it is God we carry and that it is God who is humble
enough to come to us every day in the Eucharist.

Where is the real action? If you enter the depths of your
heart and ponder God's presence in you, you will be in the
midst of the greatest activity known to humanity. You will be
in the heart of the Trinity.

"I am at peace,
knowing that our
needs are resting
quietly in the
arms of
Our Lady of
Combermere.

We can rest like
a child on it's
mothers breast,
knowing her
mantle of love
and protection is
over each of us."

The Little Mandate

Arise—go! Sell all you possess. Give it directly,
    personally to the poor. Take up My cross (their
    cross) and follow Me, going to the poor, being
    poor, being one with them, one with Me.

Little—be always little! Be simple, poor, childlike.

Preach the Gospel with your life—*without compromise!*
    Listen to the Spirit. He will lead you.

Do little things exceedingly well for love of Me.

Love . . . love . . . love, never counting the cost.

Go into the marketplace and stay with Me. Pray, fast.
    Pray always, fast.

Be hidden. Be a light to your neighbour's feet. Go
    without fears into the depth of men's hearts. I
    shall be with you.

Pray always. *I will be your rest.*

Chapter I

In Our Mother's Heart

In the sixth month, the angel Gabriel was sent by God to a town in Galilee called Nazareth, to a virgin betrothed to a man named Joseph, of the House of David; and the virgin's name was Mary. He went in and said to her, "Rejoice, you who enjoy God's favor! The Lord is with you." She was deeply disturbed by these words and asked herself what this greeting could mean.

— Luke 1:26–29

Mother Mary,
You who hold us
In your heart,
Give us your tenderness.
Give us your compassion.
Give us your silence.
Give us your humility,
So that every day
We will be able to receive
The great goodness and love,
The mercy and the justice,
Of your Son
Who pours himself out
Upon all of us
For all eternity.

Who is this woman? Who is this young Jewess who heard the thunder and whisper of the Creator in the depths of her being? Patriarchs, prophets, holy men of God, who knew and lived the Jewish tradition, longed for what she heard. Mary was brought to the Temple as a child and began this mysterious journey that we've barely begun to grasp the meaning of, even after 2,000 years of Christianity.

Who is this woman who heard through the angel Gabriel, "Will you become the Mother of God?" The whole world entered into silence and hiddenness when that Yes went forth and the pregnancy of God himself entered into her being. The Incarnation began a revolution of love that continues even now—in you and me.

Are our hearts silent? Are our ears attuned to creation all around us?

Are we silent and listening to the heartbeats of our brothers and sisters? Are we standing still, listening to the all-consuming love that enters into us during the Liturgy, receiving again and again this great outpouring of love into every cell of our bodies?

This great prophetess is alive and well. Her Son comes to us over and over again. The Sanctifier is piercing and penetrating every corner of our beings, so that we can be transformed, transfigured, and restored. All we need to do is simply know that Almighty God arranges every minute of our days, whether we are in joy or pain, to bring forth in us what is humanly impossible—Jesus Christ.

In faith, we know that a seed was planted in our lives when we first consecrated ourselves to Our Lady. The seed is growing according to our unique life experiences into a greater and greater flowering of the mystery of love.

All of history changed at the Annunciation, at the moment Our Lady said, "*Fiat.*" At that moment, the cross and the crib were wed. The inevitable outcome of the history of the universe began. Today our hearts beat with expectation and joy, knowing that no matter what tomorrow brings, the end of the story is resurrection for all of us.

The human and the divine revolve around one word—the *yes* I say to God and to you.

> Every person of the apostolate has, in a manner of speaking, heard an angel speak. Each has said his or her fiat, or will say it.
>
> — Catherine Doherty

We each grow like a child in its mother's womb. Our growth is hidden, imperceptible, and often unseen. It struck me that this growth takes form in God's heart because every day we are being drawn more deeply into one body, one mind, one heart in Jesus Christ.

Our Lady is forming each of us. Her spouse, the Holy Spirit, is probing the secret chambers of our inner being and purifying them, bringing forth our uniqueness in the face of Jesus Christ.

The substance of our daily life will come forth through the leadership of the Mother of God. She is orchestrating every corner of our lives. We need only to become listening children, flexible, pliable, humble and loving in her hands, so that the glory of her Son can shine through us.

The grace to achieve what is important and needful can be given in an instant through the mercy of God. He loves us. He created us and gave us to his Mother. There is nothing we need to worry about, for that security that goes beyond anything human surrounds us night and day.

I am at peace, knowing that all of our needs are resting quietly in the hands of the Mother of God, who is our mother and in whose heart we live.

Slowly but surely, we are awakening individually and as a family, and realizing that we can rest like a child on its mother's breast, knowing that the mantle of Our Lady's love and protection is over each one of us, to bring to completion in us the great calling in life given to each of us.

This is Our Lady's age. She is forming us in her Son's glory, letting his radiance become the light of our countenance.

Our Lady's apparitions have reached astounding numbers throughout the world. Our Lady's presence pushes each of us to come closer to, and to trust more in her loving maternal protection. She is the person who steps on the Evil One, bringing about the ultimate triumph of her Immaculate Heart.

At the Basilica of Our Lady of Guadalupe in Mexico City in 1999, Pope John Paul II elevated Our Lady of Guadalupe's feast day to a solemnity. The Holy Father proclaimed her to be the empress of all the Americas.

This message went deep into my heart and I said to God, "Does this mean that the Holy Father is telling us of the ultimate triumph of the Immaculate Heart of Mary—she who is destined to crush the head of the Evil One with her heel? Is this a prophetic utterance that is foreshadowing a glorious restoration that we cannot see as yet?"

Let us pray that this is so.

We belong to Our Lady so that she can bring forth the life of Jesus in each of us. The Father chose this way for the Christianization of the world. We must never forget that Our Lady is the person who nurtures us, loves us, forms us, teaches us, so that we become unique and irreplaceable icons of Jesus Christ.

> She is also the one who, precisely as the "handmaid of the Lord," cooperates unceasingly with the work of salvation accomplished by Christ, her Son.
>
> — John Paul II, *Redemptoris Mater*

The popular spiritual writer, Father Basil Pennington, noted in his work *Mary Today: The Challenging Woman*[1], "One day I picked up a little booklet from a stand near the door of our college hall and stuck it into my pocket. A few days later when I was riding a bus on Staten Island I pulled it out and began reading. That was January 1951. That reading changed the course of my life. The booklet was Louis de Montfort's *Secret of Mary*. It argued for entrusting ourselves completely to Mary as Jesus had done in his conception, childhood, and youth. Four days later I did that. In the language of de Montfort, I consecrated myself to Mary. Less than five months later, I found myself in her monastery and I was given the name Mary. Five years

1. M. Basil Pennington, *Mary Today: The Challenging Woman* (Garden City NY: Doubleday, 1987)

later I would be consecrated a monk by the Church on the day honoring her birth."

The gospel is universal. Jesus Christ is calling each one of us every day. His Mother is the one who leads us to him through a simple, maternal compassion.

Frank Duff, founder of the Legion of Mary, said that there was a direct connection between the Legion's development and their discovery of St. Louis de Montfort's classic work, *True Devotion to the Blessed Virgin*. Their small group had tried for some time to get the Legion off the ground. After making the de Montfort consecration to Jesus through Mary, they experienced phenomenal growth. Frank Duff said, "It is impossible to believe that the connection between the *True Devotion* discovery and the immediate emergence of the Legion of Mary at the next monthly meeting was a coincidence."

Mary brings us together, giving us holy strength, courage, and wisdom. Through her faithful surrender, a dying secular, materialistic world is brought to life in her Son. Each moment that we wrap ourselves in her merciful mantle of love, we let life and light into a world weary of death and darkness.

We are being asked to let go of our typical ways of dealing with life. We are being asked by God himself to place our feet on an unknown and unseen road. We are asked to walk hand in hand. This requires great trust. God is faithful. He is asking us to make a huge leap into the valley of faith. This is impossible for humans to achieve except through the mercy of God himself.

Now is my time and your time, the time for all Christians to surrender to Jesus totally, irrevocably, as he surrendered for us. Only love can do that sort of surrendering. Only love can make that surrender a way of life. Surrender is another way of saying *commitment*.

In order to live the Christian life, we must desire with our whole heart, with our whole soul, and with our whole mind, to be sanctified. We must hunger to give our whole lives as Our Lady did for the salvation of souls. We make a difference, not because of who we are, but because God lives in all of us.

When we take or renew our consecration, let none of us look back. Rather with childlike trust and confidence let us enter together into the heart of the Mother of God. We take our consecration as a family. Let the *I* in all of us become the *we* of our oneness and love.

Read and reread the gospel of St. John where our Lord prayed that we all be one:

"May they all be one, just as, Father, you are in me and I am in you, so that they also may be in us, so that the world may believe it was you who sent me.

"I have given them the glory you gave to me, that they may be one as we are one.

"With me in them and you in me, may they be so perfected in unity that the world will recognize that it was you who sent me and that you have loved them as you have loved me."[2]

The heart of our family life depends on our oneness with the Holy Trinity. We are being formed by the Mother of God who had the Trinity in her heart from the moment of the Annunciation. With our *fiat*, this grace is extended down through history to us. That is why we consecrate ourselves to her. She will do in silence and hiddenness what we cannot do for ourselves. The big word for all of us is *trust*.

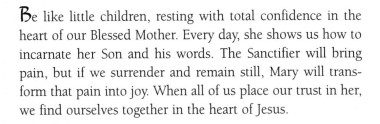

Be like little children, resting with total confidence in the heart of our Blessed Mother. Every day, she shows us how to incarnate her Son and his words. The Sanctifier will bring pain, but if we surrender and remain still, Mary will transform that pain into joy. When all of us place our trust in her, we find ourselves together in the heart of Jesus.

God the Father created man. From Adam's rib, he created woman. God the Father, through the angel Gabriel, asked

2. John 17:21–23

Mary to be the mother of his Son, the Mother of God. From the woman, the man-God came into being. She is all love—the Immaculate Conception.

If you seek love, you must go to her as children and drink from her tenderness and wisdom. Take your fears and hatreds, in all their various negative forms, to her. Talk to her. Let her love you, so that your broken nature can be filled and restored with her tender love. Only then will you be able to absorb the heights and depths of the words of her Son. Without her, you will not know what his words mean in their profundity, in their interior life-giving power.

Who will bring forth this new creation in us? Call upon the Holy Spirit with verve and confidence. Allow the Holy Spirit to penetrate, to reveal all the untruths in your mind and heart. Step by step, take your maladies of hatred, fear, anger, and resentment to the Mother of God, and she will gently and quietly give you the security and safety that you desire.

Little by little, when we stop blaming, judging, and criticizing one another, we find that everything we seek is already in our hearts. We discover that we are, in a sense, already home, for the beauty and extraordinary peace that we hunger and thirst for is already in our hearts.

Remember that it is not pain, suffering and emotional disturbance that is the essence of our being. Our souls carry the very presence of the Father, the Son, and the Holy Spirit.

By our consecration, we are led night and day by the Mother of God. Every day, she is leading us and forming us in the interior of our beings, unveiling the true icons that we were created to be from time immemorial. She is leading us into the perfection willed by God the Father at the moment of our conceptions.

This morning I asked Our Lady, "What are you doing with us?" Suddenly, like a flash of blinding light, I saw her in an event in history that turned creation around. It was Our Lady of the Annunciation. The words, *"Let it be done unto me according to your word,"* suddenly exploded in my heart. For Our Lady at that moment, there was a lightning impenetration of the Holy Spirit, into her silence, into her hiddenness.

It was a light so powerful that it made the atomic bomb appear like a dim firefly on a dark night. Is it possible to grasp what took place?

Then I saw Our Lady and the Apostles gathered in the Upper Room, trembling, weakened, poverty-stricken, because the Master had left them, and they had only fear in their hearts. At this *Pentecost*, once again a blinding explosion took place. It gave a body of men the courage to go forth to bring the great news that Jesus Christ, their Savior, was alive and well.

> *Christ's Mother—who was present at the beginning of "the time of the Church," when in expectation of the coming of the Holy Spirit she devoted herself to prayer in the midst of the Apostles and her Son's disciples—constantly 'precedes' the Church in her journey through human history.*
>
> — John Paul II,
> *Redemptoris Mater*

There are hidden and silent signs of Our Lady moving quietly and relentlessly across the face of the earth. Certainly our own love for Our Lady has grown over the years. It is seldom that anyone coming to Madonna House doesn't make a point of going to the shrine of Our Lady of Combermere, leaving with her whatever burdens, petitions, or thanksgiving they have. She is our mother, and we are becoming more and more like little children as we approach her with all of the things that are insolvable in our own hearts.

The earth is covered with this year's first snowfall. It has deepened and intensified the silence of God, reflected in his creation. We are all moving into that time of the year when waiting, expectation, and promise of fulfillment is upon us— a time when Our Lady, with St. Joseph, brings us into the birth of Christ.

The silence of the season leads my heart to Nazareth. Not just the geographic spot but the place that must be in all of our hearts.

This morning as I was praying to Catherine about unity, she responded very quickly. We often talk about what truly unifies us in the Body of Christ. Then I found in her writings what Catherine says about God's Mandate to her:

"The spirit of Madonna House is 'the spirit of Nazareth.' It is to be humble and hidden. It is to be poor in earthly goods, having only the necessities. This spirit should lead all belonging to Madonna House to a detachment from one's will, to a detachment of heart—especially from one's possessions, family, friends, and country. This should be done in a manner that will lead one to find all of these in the heart of Christ.

"We 'preach the Gospel with our life.' We do 'little things with a great love' of God and neighbor. We are a 'family' like the one in Nazareth, a family of God, hence a community of charity or love. We believe that we must be before the Lord first, and do for the Lord next. We bear witness to God in 'the marketplaces' of the world. We identify with those we serve."

What does the tiny, hidden town of Nazareth mean for us today? It means beginning again. It means letting our wounded, sinful hearts lead us home—to a Mother totally alive, serving her Son. It means discovering where the gospel got its start and getting another chance to live it. It means returning to simply living in the true light. What good can come from Nazareth? Fear not—a new creation!

No one is finished with transformation. We finish when we die, and then we will see God face to face in all his glory and be eternally blessed. Until then, we have lots of inner work to do, and plenty of outer building of this house of love.

A Call to Love

The angel said to her,
"Mary, do not be afraid; you have won God's
favor. Look! You are to conceive in your womb
and bear a son, and you must name him Jesus.
He will be great and will be called
Son of the Most High. The Lord God will
give him the throne of his ancestor David;
he will rule over the House of Jacob forever
and his reign will have no end.

— Luke 1:30–33

Lord, give us the eyes

  to see how much your love is

    knocking at the door of our hearts for others.

Give us hearts that will sing

  with gratitude and praise

    for everything that happens to us.

Give us hearts that will say *thank you*

  at the beginning of the day

    and say *thank you for this day*

      when our eyes are closing for sleep at night.

In the early '70s, Catherine Doherty said to me, pointing to a poustinia on the island in Combermere, "Now you know about it. Go open a 'poustinia in the marketplace.'" So, she sent me to open the first prayer listening house—a poustinia in the market place—for Madonna House. Since her book, *Poustinia*, hadn't yet been published, few people knew this word or this work.

I was sent to a city where we'd recently closed an apostolate, to a neighborhood not interested in my mission. I went in obedience, trusting that this was God's will. But, fear was brewing in me. It cast a chill through me those first few days. So much so that at night, I would crawl into bed and turn up the electric blanket even though it was temperate there compared to Canadian winter. I wondered if I could find the faith that Catherine had, the faith that moved her to throw somebody like me into a situation like this.

Many people prayed for this mission, and little by little, doors opened.

The first few days, I stayed at a local convent. Then, someone from the diocese took me to lunch and asked what I was about. Over a hamburger and coffee, he listened to the cry of my heart, and then he asked for my credentials. I showed him my only credential, a 3×5 card called "The Little Mandate." He found us an ideal house for $82.50 a month, and the rent never changed. It turned out that he was a former Friendship House[1] person.

We, who live in an apostolate that gives away everything, soon began to realize that whatever we needed mysteriously showed up. Linens, food, a toaster, cleaning supplies, everything to make a home appeared without us specifically begging for them. But only what we needed came; we received one spatula, not two. Seeing these household items come from the poor, the middle class, the not so middle class, floored me. I stood in the middle of that house one day and cried out to God, "Forgive me for not having faith." I've never forgotten how God provided for us down to our miniscule needs.

I even once said to my fellow staff worker, Kim, "We need our lawn cut. We don't have a lawnmower. What are we going to do?" Then I heard myself say, "I know what we are going to do!" We went to the chapel, knelt before the Blessed Sacrament like children, and prayed, "Jesus, we need our grass cut. Please help us."

Some men who ran a soup kitchen had invited us to breakfast. We didn't know them. When we met, the head of the group asked, "Do you need anything?"

"We need our grass cut," I said.

"This afternoon I'll send two fellows out to do that," he responded.

Do you have faith? Do you believe?

---

1. Catherine Doherty founded Friendship House prior to Madonna House.

God takes care of everything if we trust him.

I believe with all my heart that God is bending over each of us and asking, "What do you need?" Not "What do you want?" but "What do you need?" God is saying, "I am here. I am your Father. I have promised you. Come to me. Ask me. Trust me."

> Go forth as an apostle—with no shoes, no gold or silver. Then you too will hear the words of Christ at the end of the journey, "Have you wanted for anything?"
>
> — Catherine Doherty

You and I must become saints, nothing less. This is our Savior's work. We must work with him each day to purify the parts within us that don't love and serve others. We must die to selfishness.

You are called to be a saint. The Suffering Christ stands before you and calls you. We are all called to be saints, to love and serve everyone, all people, regardless of who they are. Let us join hands so that the transcendent gospel of our Lord and Savior Jesus Christ can reach those who are hungry for faith, hope, love, and the restoration of authentic peace on earth.

To walk with sure feet, clear eyes, and courage, we need to pray every day for faith, hope, and love. Passions and emotions camouflage our core reality, our inner being. They separate us from the Trinity who dwells within us. As we get in touch with our core reality, our inner being, we hasten our liberation and freedom.

Our Lord and Savior Jesus Christ seems to be weaning us from false securities and idols, so that we can cling to him alone. Keep in mind, God permits things to happen to us so that we can grow in faith. We desire with our whole heart to give our life to Jesus Christ. Only through his gift of self can we give ourselves to one another. The choice for God takes place in the human heart. Every day we must decide that our life is only for Jesus Christ. Everything else flows from that.

Expect miracles. Expect grace upon grace to come into your life. Stay faithful to the "duty of the moment." It is your guiding beacon of faith.

We're not called to an ordinary life but to a supernatural life lived in the ordinary.

The deepest level of reality in our lives is God's will for us, and the fleshing out of his will in daily life.

All of us are being touched by God directly, individually, with the light that the Holy Spirit gives to each, for both our inward and outward journeys. In our common life, we must be watchful of these two areas and see that the common good takes precedent over the individual good, and that the external structures stay external so the interior structures can be centered on God alone.

As we move through our daily work, we can remember that we have consumed Jesus Christ in the Eucharist. He remains present in us through our baptism and he strengthens his life in us through all the sacraments, for we ask him to live and dwell in us.

Think about what one person—who really believes—can do, in silence and hiddenness, to transform the world.

Your hands are holy because you carry God. Your words are sacred because you carry God. In order to have all your hunger and thirst filled, you are dependent only upon the bountiful and endless flow of love being poured out upon you every day.

Catherine frequently wrote about the salvation of souls. She emphasized the profound mystery hidden within each member of the mystical body of Christ. The presence of our Lord remains in us through the Eucharist.

Our broken humanity and the nitty-gritty grating of daily life blind us to what is taking place during the Liturgy. The Eucharist is the source and center of our life. Pray about this, discuss this with other people, so that your soul can drink in more fully from the rich reality in one single Mass.

A woman by the name of Frances Murray had a powerful influence on me during my teenage years. She was a close friend of my mother and father. Frances' mother died when she was three years old. Her father was an alcoholic. Her grandmother raised her and infused a powerful faith into her mind and heart. From our modern stance, we would say that this woman coming from a broken home didn't stand a chance of living a decent life.

Perhaps it was the gentler circumstances of intact family life and stable parish life in that pre-1960 world that allowed her to live as she did. She never married. She was a nurse of exceptional ability. She often visited our family on Sundays. She was always with us on Christmas, Easter, and Thanksgiving. She had no immediate family. We became her center for that kind of fulfillment. How clearly I remember her vibrant, enthusiastic, and life-giving energy.

This woman was a daily communicant. She poured her life out for the poorest of the poor. She was vitally interested in everyone and everything. Her voluntary poverty, which was totally unnecessary, seemed, in those days, a bit strange. Nothing mattered to her, even when more materialistic and prosperous people would nudge her in a different direction. She lived in the midst of everyone, and yet you could tell she lived by some secret, silent code that was never verbally expressed.

She had an appendectomy when I was fourteen and came to our house to recuperate. One day, unbeknownst to her, I went upstairs. When I stepped into the hallway, I caught sight of her sitting up in bed. She had a look on her face of such radiance and joy that the sight has remained fresh in my memory all these years. Her face in that moment was like a piercing arrow from the Holy Spirit. It pierced my heart causing me to ponder the soul-searching question, "How does that kind of joy come to anyone?"

As a teenager the preoccupation with self, the struggle to find my place in the world, consumed me. But that memory haunted me through the years.

I now know that this woman was a walking incarnation of the presence of Jesus Christ. She loved, prayed, and laid her life down for countless people. In my memory, I see her zeal and vitality walking beside me. No doubt she was one of those silent prayers who became a *tour de force* in my own conversion.

We're part of that silent, hidden army of people who carry in our flesh the Body and Blood of Jesus Christ through our baptism and the daily feeding of that life through the Eucharist. How blessed we are to be able to go to the altar of God, the God who gives joy to our youth!

No one talked about the sacramental life when I was a child. We simply did our duty by attending Sunday Mass, saying our prayers, and measuring up to the letter of the law. This woman, who took the interior meaning of all of that very seriously, and who undoubtedly suffered from the mediocre standards that came from the world, had a revolutionary effect upon my own life in God. Perhaps I can be bold enough to say this hidden saint is multiplied in many corners of the world, unknown and unheralded by others.

We too can be this unquenchable source of life for others simply by believing and by feeding that belief through the presence of Jesus Christ who loves us far beyond anything we can hope for or imagine.

Let us make a resolution to be gentle with one another, to speak words that build one another's confidence and trust, to see only what is godly in one another, and guard our thoughts against any accusations that can wound again today that bleeding body of Jesus Christ. We are restorers of life, first within our own hearts, then with one another, and then for the whole world. I pray that we all decrease and that the humble, majestic Christ will increase in each one of us, through the power of the sanctifying presence of the Holy Spirit.

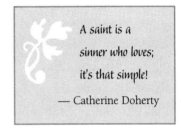

A saint is a sinner who loves; it's that simple!

— Catherine Doherty

Through Baptism we are plunged into the life, death, and resurrection of Jesus Christ.

We are the temples of the Holy Spirit. God lives in us.

What was hidden is being unearthed. The seed and truth of Jesus Christ have been planted in each of us. Each of us must declare, I will live, I will love, I will serve, I will be an icon of the Lord Jesus Christ.

When the Holy Father, John Paul II, pronounced these phrases, "The culture of life . . . the culture of death," he encapsulated the titanic cosmic struggle between love and hate, light and darkness, life and death.

We, who carry the living God in us, must have the courage, peace, joy, and confidence to simply throw our lives into the heart of love, no matter what tomorrow brings. We must pray for the leaders of nations, pray for all of those who have the responsibility of leading people.

Yesterday's Liturgy gave us these words, "I offer you life or death."[2] It's a simple choice—one that will be with us until we leave this earth. It is a choice shot through with the joy and glory of the cross—restored forever through resurrection.

> On this journey we are accompanied by the Blessed Virgin Mary to whom . . . in the presence of a great number of Bishops assembled in Rome from all parts of the world, I entrusted the Third Millennium. . . . I have invoked her as the "Star of the New Evangelization."
>
> — John Paul II,
> *Novo Millennio Ineunte*

This is the beginning of a new millennium. No Christian today can be asleep, compromised, or complacent about anything. The life and death of the globe, to say nothing of billions of souls, is at stake.

The use of New Age modalities to try and heal people who are desperate is increasing. If the public is not properly informed about the danger of this, people can be afflicted with negative spiritual influences and consequences, even though they initially receive a healing.

In this day and age when materialism and individualism rage like prairie fires, we need to extinguish those tendencies in ourselves. We all have them. To flesh out what it means to be a disciple of Jesus Christ, requires interior and exterior discipline. And so, we return again and again to the basic princi-

2. Deuteronomy 30:19

ples of our communal life. We must continue this until the day we die.

Every stage in our spiritual and human development requires reworking, re-looking, and reevaluating. Those who are older have different needs from those who are younger. There are different stages of being transformed by the gospel. So we need to communicate with our spiritual directors. All of us must be accountable to God, to other people, and to ourselves, no matter who or where we are. Then life will bring us light, joy, peace, and love.

When God chooses someone for the consecrated life, the meeting between God and this person is impossible to put into words. When Jesus walked the earth he said, "Do not judge and you will not be judged."[3] He must have been seeing through time, seeing how the Church would be battered by shallow words, seeing how difficult forces would try to break apart the mystery, try to reduce it to paltry human terms. Let us fast from this superficiality. Let us honor, respect, and bow before one another. Let us praise the workings of God.

The spiritual life is total and complete. It contradicts the secular humanistic world that has infected us.

Do not rely on your own cleverness, your own light. Rather, beg God to take from you anything that does not allow his kingdom to come into your daily life. Give your all! Grace will be given in abundance. If you give yourself fully and work to be faithful to the duty of the moment, a trail of

3. Matthew 7:1

light will flow from you, invisibly touching everyone you meet.

Catherine often said that the heart of the difficulty in the world is not the economic, political, or cultural circumstances that surround us, but the division between good and evil, the division between life and death, a division in our own hearts. So we need to return again and again to the heart of the matter found at the crossroads of our freedom. This crossroads is identified in Deuteronomy 30:15–20. At its core, God says, "I am offering you life or death, blessing or curse. Choose life, then, so that you and your descendants may live in the love of Yahweh, your God."[4]

The domain of the inner being called "free will" is the sacred domain of each individual. No one can touch the will. This is the uniqueness of being human—God allows us to choose between life and death. Every morning when we awake we must choose life, choose to live, choose to love, choose to serve. We must choose, every day, and perhaps several times during the day, in order to grow in grace, in truth, and in the fullness of life, as promised by our Lord and Savior Jesus Christ.

On this walk, we must have a passion for truth, a passion for forgiveness, a passion for trusting that God is with us and will give us a thousandfold what we need.

Only God will be our rest. In the meantime we struggle against mediocrity, our private kingdoms, our resistance to the mercy of God.

---

4. Deuteronomy 30:19

When faced with oppression, I resort to this advice:
Read the Psalms persistently.
Make repeated acts of faith.
Love and trust.
Avoid focusing on feelings.
Laugh in the face of the foe.
Let the body do what the spirit can't.
Pray with praise and adoration.
Rest in the hearts of Our Lady and her Son.

We will only know and understand in heaven what our individual and collective life has meant to the spreading of the kingdom.

Jesus fills us with a love that grows. It increases, for ourselves and for each other. Through it we surrender all that we are and all that we hope to be. Like little children, we run into his Mother's arms first. This is how family life grows in God's family.

We live the hidden life, because Our Lady, her Son, and Joseph lived the hidden life in Bethlehem and Nazareth. For 30 years, their life was not known, not heralded, not understood. Then, our Lord's public life was filled with manifestations, miracles, teachings, with moving people's hearts. In the end, it was filled with rejection. Finally, he was lead to Golgotha. Why? To proclaim the greatest love that ever lived. He said *yes* to his Father, just as his Mother had said *yes* to him 33 years before. Jesus' *fiat* to his Father was *thy will, not mine be done*. He spoke his *fiat* in the midst of an unbearable realization of what was facing him. His *fiat* became our freedom.

Each of us has been chosen by the Father, the Son, the Holy Spirit, to say *yes* as Our Lady did. For she is the one who forms us. She makes it possible for us through ordinary, humble, simple daily life to be emptied in a way that we cannot even begin to imagine.

If we are faithful and surrender every day, a deep mysterious hidden work takes place in each one of our hearts. This work is known only to God. A fire comes forth from it. It burns, burns, and burns. It goes forth to the far corners of the world. It touches people in ways possible only through grace.

If we totally give ourselves, God takes that sacrifice and transmits love to other people through our offering. Nothing, nothing is ever wasted when our hearts and the heart of God beat together in that cradle of love, mercy, and tenderness.

One of the cardinal facets of our lives is our call to walk in the darkness of faith.

Are you afraid of pain? Why? Pain is not a punishment. Pain is a symptom. Pain is nature's way of saying "something is not right; something needs correcting." If my tooth aches, I go to the dentist. If my head aches, I take an aspirin.

Do you hunger for holiness, for life? Do you thirst to love and be loved?

Are you tormented by the interior struggle to be freed from the chains of sin and death that are part of your inheritance as a human?

Are you begging God for mercy? Are you asking the Holy Spirit for the light of truth and love to pierce the inner darkness that you wrestle with?

Are you afraid of death, afraid to live, hiding from your neighbor? Why?

Are you pouring out your life for others?

Why do these questions burn within me? They burn because something is happening. A light is coming into the world. The invitation of love is being extended to each of us.

A phrase thundered in my heart when I awakened this morning. *Be still, and know that I am God!*[5]

Our God is mercy. God cares. God is active and alive in you and will never abandon you. These are merely words, but to grasp them takes *faith*.

The great gift that Catherine gave us is faith. Without faith we cannot hope, and without hope we cannot truly love one another. The gospel invites us to love. This means going beyond what we can achieve as human beings.

We know that faith is a gift. We know that we receive it at our baptism. We know that as we mature into adulthood, we have to assent over and over again to this gift of faith.

We begin our journey into the heart of God with a *yes*. Subsequently we must say "Yes" again and again until the full stature of Jesus Christ is moving so powerfully in us, with us, and through us, that we no longer desire anything but the will of the Father.

We know in faith that this struggle never stops until we see God face to face. But every time we go through a trial or a temptation and we cling with firmness and resolve to the

5. Psalm 46:10 (NIV)

faith, we die a little, spiritually. We become more and more detached, more and more free from being obsessed with our own ideas, our own passions. We become strengthened by the presence of the living God within us.

Perhaps the most difficult journey we have is that of coming to the realization that faith goes beyond human reason, that we are men and women of faith and must learn to fold the wings of our intellect.

Strangely, we must lose our spiritual eyesight and hearing and even become dumb and speechless, all for faith and in faith. We must journey into a land of unknowing darkness, because we love and believe in God who is love. We are never alone. For enclosed within us live the three persons—Father, Son, and Holy Spirit.

Our passion to love God with our whole heart, our whole mind, and our whole soul will grow in each of us as we take each step in faith. Each step taken in trust and self-giving fuses our minds and hearts. Although everyone is at a different stage on the journey, we experience a unity. One by one we encounter our collective heart. The urgency of Christ keeps us moving.

We must remind ourselves of our Catholic heritage, we must find out what part of the gospel path God is reminding us of, when things crop up in daily life that make us uneasy, when we're perplexed by one another's choices or behavior.

Joy and pain are part of the tapestry that allows God to be our all in all. Trust! Trust as never before to be formed and restored according to the gospel's promise, not in what the world knows to be restoration.

Learn to love pain and joy. Learn to love every day, no matter what it brings. Trust that the Almighty is working in and through you, in ways you will only understand in time to come.

Throw away your fears, throw away your controls, throw away everything that binds you and limits your vision of God's love for you. Pray to be free. Pray to see Jesus in your brothers and sisters. Pray to glory in his goodness as it comes to you every day in the quiet moments that seem so small yet are so full of glory.

I came across this passage among Catherine's correspondences with Father Furfey, her spiritual director in the late '30s and early '40s:

"The soul of the apostolate is death to self.

"The journey inward has been long. The end is not far and only now do I begin to understand and see.

"Oh, Father, how tragic it is that it took me years to get here. How silly that I did not see that little else matters except my inner path.

"I've always loved God. I've always known that love is pain and sacrifice. But he showed me that love is death, and that death is life.

"Old words. Repeated ad nauseum via spiritual writings. Words read and reread. Commented on by me with the foolish pride of human wisdom. I thought I knew what these words meant.

"It took many blows to crush me to earth, many cuts to make me bleed. And even while bleeding, I needed to recognize that wounds are only a part of surrender. I had to be slapped around to come to my senses.

"Amen and Alleluia! God be blessed for that pain.

"For all the bitterness it brought me. Alleluia!"

Catherine Doherty's recurring eternal theme was *God became man so that man could become one with God*. Divinization! She wove and rewove the story of Jesus Christ, the endless layers demonstrating this simple meaning contained in each word of Scripture, never deviating from this cycle of life.

Jesus is the gospel. You're called to fully incarnate him, and this will be your call until you become one with him, until you see him face to face.

Chapter I I I

Letting God

*Mary said to the angel, "But how can this come
about, since I have no knowledge of man?"
The angel answered, "The Holy Spirit will come
upon you, and the power of the Most High will
cover you with its shadow. And so the child will
be holy and will be called Son of God. And I tell
you this too: your cousin Elizabeth also, in her
old age, has conceived a son, and she whom
people called barren is now in her sixth month,
for nothing is impossible to God."*

— Luke 1:34–37

Our own heart
is the first mission field.
The restoration of our own world
begins by
simply being before God.

In this era of families torn asunder, of wars and rumors of
wars, of people trembling with fear of bombs and planes
falling from the sky, of worry over life-destroying microorganisms spreading through our water or air, it is a relief to be
wrapped in the silence and presence of the Mother of God.
She watches over her children as we falter or hesitate on our
journey in staying faithful to her Son. She is eternally soothing us, holding us, and whispering words of consolation and
tenderness into us.

Pause to contemplate and appreciate that it was the
Mother of God who carried the Lord Jesus Christ in her
womb for nine months. She was the first to have his physical
presence inside of her body. What he gave to her none of us
can begin to comprehend. But we who are the followers of
Our Lady in this journey consume Christ daily in the
Eucharist.

Ponder the Eucharist during these days. This is a time of
waiting, of silence, of expectation, but Christ was enfolded
not only in the womb of Our Lady 2,000 years ago, he is spiritually present in you. In faith, contemplate this gift. We must
believe with a faith we have never seen before in the history
of Christianity.

If we could see with our human eyes what happens at the
moment of the consecration of ordinary bread and wine into
the Body and Blood of Jesus Christ, we would fall flat on our

faces with joy, adoration, and praise. Know that the Lord who was present in Our Lady's womb is just as present in our bodies when we receive him in the Eucharist. After receiving the Eucharist, take a few minutes to allow him to consume every cell of your body, so that in the days ahead you no longer live but only he will live in you. The Eucharist is with us, *God is with us.*

As a page of history turns, we must live our days in this coming time ever mindful of who we carry, who humbly comes to us daily through the Eucharist. You, *you,* carry God. Where is the real action? Enter the depths of your heart— ponder God's presence in you, and you will be at the heart of the greatest activity known to man. You will be in the heart of the Trinity.

The Father knows us, and his Son came to give us everything we need to be happy. He came to fill us and restore us to what his Father desired us to be when we were conceived.

Nothing is impossible for God. But unless we open our hearts, we will wander down the endless roads of our own human thinking and emotional entanglements, never finding our way to glory, which is God himself.

The most important thing we can do is open our hearts to receive God's love, for God desires to love us, and desires to live in us.

Only God will see us through. Fear, worry, or trust in false forms of security will not. Only by trusting in Jesus Christ who is incarnating his gospel through us, will we experience the immense and glorious restoration of his kingdom on earth.

Today there is no longer a human solution to the problems of our catastrophic world, beset by the rapidly mounting escalation of powers and principalities. The only solution comes from the heart of God himself. We little ones, who know that God's mercy is with us each moment, must fall down in thanksgiving, praise, and adoration.

> When the Lord consecrates persons, he gives them a special grace so that they can fulfill his will of love.
>
> — John Paul II,
> Lineamenta

Regrettably, we tend to seek security from ourselves or those around us. And it doesn't work. Exercise your faith and trust, not in people but in God. God must be first—God alone. Pray before the Blessed Sacrament like a child. And there you will learn not to hurt yourself or others.

We must let go of our humanistic approaches to solving our problems of living together with others. Then we will be free to realize the intimacy and unity we hunger for in the Eucharist.

Everyone seeks stability.
    We look for greater values than the world's towers of

Babel. We look for values that keep us off the rapid treadmills of faddish change fostered by modern communication technologies.

We need to discover how to stand still and trust in God's living presence within us—to listen with confidence in our hearts to God's Word. Then we will open ourselves to the love he has for each of us. In this way the Father works through each of us revealing the gospel of his Son.

It is important that we have confidence that he will use us through our words, silence, and perhaps our prayers uttered for another's consolation.

It is exciting to be alive in this way! What extraordinary times we live in. We can see the parting of the sea and beyond. We can see through the powers and principalities of death to those of life.

Choose life! And you will gain love and truth. Choose your baptismal life as never before.

We're up against not only powers and principalities, but also what the world calls perfection. This is not the perfection that our heavenly Father seeks through fidelity to his Son.

Doing the little things well with great love will allow us to become a mighty David, able to overcome the giant Goliaths of a sinful, violent world.

Do not fall into the traps of a self-fulfillment offered by the world. Our salvation comes from Jesus Christ. He is our Savior.

God is the final answer.

Jesus Christ died and rose, becoming the ultimate answer to every struggle in the world.

I heard these words over the radio, "The same power that raised Jesus from the dead lives and reigns in you."

What do you choose today? To live according to your kingdom? Or to love according to God's kingdom? Every choice of every day is crucial.

Without prayer all we do remains only human, possessing perhaps a thin veneer of charity. Without prayer we do not enter the depths of the Triune God.

> Real zeal is standing still and letting God be a bonfire in you.
>
> — Catherine Doherty

The Holy Spirit moves us into living prayer, individually and communally, ultimately to the deep levels where *sobornost*[1] lies.

We must be restored as much as possible to our baptismal innocence, for without God we are nothing and can do nothing. But with God all things are possible. When we believe, he will fulfill his every word. Therefore let us pray each day, "Thy Kingdom come, Thy will be done on earth as it is in heaven." Let us, through faith and trust in God, bring his kingdom into each present moment.

---

1. *Sobornost* is a Russian word Catherine used to indicate total unity of mind and heart that comes through the Trinity. Baptism plunges us into unity with the Trinity and with one another.

When you pray remember that God the Father, Son, and Holy Spirit and Mary the Mother of God are persons—alive and active in your life. Talk to them as persons. Drop mumbling dutifully pious prayers and speak to them, listen to them, converse with them. This is prayer. By praying to the persons of God, you will find that the hunger and desire to be one with them will grow and grow like a raging fire in your heart.

Each day pray for an increase of one of the theological virtues—faith, hope, or charity.

Pray not just individually but as part of Christ's unified body. Pray in solidarity with the whole Church. In this way we learn to hope in what God is doing, not just personally in and for each of us, but in and for all of us together.

After this hope comes love. We are called to move together, to move with a greater confidence, not in ourselves, but in God, to move toward that center of love, toward Christ.

In this way we become a bonfire that lights up the dark corners of the earth. The light perhaps will only be seen by those with spiritual eyes, with eyes for the invisible, with eyes of the Holy Spirit. We must grow and grow and grow. We must hope, and keep moving while standing still.

In the first part of your prayer, praise God. In the second part, ask the Lord to let you know what to pray for. This requires listening. In the third part, take on the intention that he gives you. Lift up that prayer to him. Do this simply when you awaken in the morning, and before the Blessed Sacrament whenever you can. This is one way you learn to live by the inspiration of the Holy Spirit day by day.

Go into the depths of your heart. And there, ponder not your own thoughts, but his thoughts. Wed your thoughts to his. Be alert and watchful every moment of every day. You are being formed minute by minute, task by task, challenge by challenge.

Be alert! Be watchful! Pray! Don't try to understand everything. Trust that you will get exactly what you need, as long as your trust is in Jesus Christ, Son of the Living God.

> Christ did not conceal from his listeners the need for suffering. . . . It is he himself who acts at the heart of human sufferings through his Spirit. . . . It is he who transforms . . . the spiritual life, indicating for the person who suffers a place close to himself.
>
> — John Paul II,
> *Salvifici Doloris*

There is a wonderful pain—the purifying fire of the Holy Spirit. It works in us, cleansing us and stripping us of all that is not of God. The pain that comes to us for our good is a treasure beyond measure. We should never turn our backs on it. For along with it comes the fire of the Holy Spirit, deepening our spiritual espousal with the Blessed Trinity.

Do not be surprised if pain, discouragement, and interior darkness suddenly blossom in you. Through pain, God purifies us to heal those parts of us that have not yet yielded to his mercy. Enter into this realm of faith with confidence and joy.

Our days are filled with light and darkness, pain and joy. Faith is the beacon that shines in the darkness of our lives. One by one we are being emptied as never before to be filled with the fire of God's love.

We are called to rejoice in poverty and in our hiddenness, to thank God for our littleness. For out of our weakness, our being stripped and emptied of all that the Western world deems important, we find joy. Ultimately, we find consolation, not grief. For through the sorrow of the cross, God lives in us and claims us, radiating his presence through us all.

No matter what you are suffering at this moment, stand still, and say a free and simple, "Yes" to God. Make this act of faith every day. In this way, you'll grow in hope and love. The Martha part of our life isn't being challenged, the Mary part is. We are the body of a crucified Christ. We suffer with his universal church, and with the world. The outpouring of love will be demanded from us more and more. Our response must be a simple, "Yes."

During our Corpus Christi procession, you could feel the presence of Jesus leading our woe-begotten crowd in triumph and simplicity. This devotion took root in peasant life long ago and far away. Walking humbly behind the monstrance reminds us of how our Lord asks us to carry him within us, and how he waits for us in silence to come to him in adoration and praise. The awesome reality of the Eucharist must take root in our minds and hearts.

We are children of our age. The barnacles of individualism and self-centered perfectionism must be scraped off us, or we weak vessels will capsize and sink (under our own weight) beneath the sea of modern life. Under these incrustations lies our capacity to simply be.

Every day, the pulse of our unity stays close to my mind and heart—not because of our desire for unity, but because of the overwhelming urgency of the Trinity to make us one within their interpersonal circle of love—Lover, Beloved, and Love. Without God, we can do nothing. Every little step toward the Trinity carries us closer to self-forgetfulness, to substituting a "we" for an "I," to approaching something incredibly hopeful happening within the family of our universal Church.

If we are unified in love for one another, we can do anything. The scriptures tell us that ultimately it's not our love for God, but God's love for us that truly matters. Therefore to fully incarnate the gospel, we must totally surrender our hearts to him. Then we'll have listening hearts, hearts at peace.

To live by faith, we must pray for eyes that see and ears that hear invisible things—things that are hidden from our humanity. The spirit of God is upon you, penetrating every part of your being. He is showing you how to see through his eyes, hear through his ears, live through his heart.

We have eyes to see. Let's look! We have ears to hear. Let's listen! Every day, whether things seem good or bad, let's each ask ourselves, "What is God saying to me now?"

God wants us to live in his creation which has no limits. Let's enlarge our vision, enlarge the boundaries of what we see. Let's go beyond the limits of nation, culture, and gender, to where cosmic tenderness and eternity consume us. If our point of view is negatively poised—*let us stop.* In that moment, let's beg God for his mercy so that we can enter his vast reality, where every little thing takes on the power of love, of life, of truth.

Let us rejoice and be glad. At the same time, let us grow very small and secure in the heart of our Lord and his Mother. Faith tells us that anything good that comes from us is a pure gift of their great love, mercy, and steadfastness.

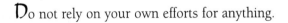

Do not rely on your own efforts for anything.

Years ago, when I was a single woman living in New York, I cried out for the Lord to show me someone or something that I could give my life to, that would have authority over my life, that I could be obedient to. I found myself being obedient in hidden ways to my employer, to my roommates, to traffic lights. Surges of joy came to me when I gave that authority to Jesus Christ, when I obeyed him.

Spiritual rebellion is pervasive today. Most drivers accept the validity of and obey without question road rules that prevent accidents. They stop at red lights, because they know that if they don't they could be killed. Why then is it so difficult to translate into the spiritual realm this simple approach to life and death?

Catherine was relentlessly obedient to her Lord, Jesus Christ. Not so much in her exterior conformity but always in her interior yielding. That was where she found her peace and love, the source of the great fruitfulness that we saw in her.

Jesus Christ is our living legitimate spiritual authority. Those persons who have authority over us are bound to be sinful, weak, and inept. But we obey them anyway and trust God to remedy any mistakes they make. When we obey them, we obey Jesus Christ through them, and life flows into us. In this way we strengthen our relationship with God.

We carry in our mind and psyche humongous wounds. When we have a conflict with someone and things hit our emotions or intellect, we must transcend the person and go to God. Within the secret chambers of our hearts, we are called to be obedient to God through that person. When we obey, whatever the situation, trust and healing come. Our obedience in faith heals us, and grace pours out in abundance through it.

Our fears are our greatest stumbling blocks. It isn't easy to face those fears. Since we were children, our psyches and senses have been bombarded with fear by our secular culture.

This makes our lives a far more difficult struggle. It robs us of our love and peace.

It is a difficult time in history. But, when we believe and trust in God, nothing can stop his expanding presence within us. The presence of God in us increases only to the degree that we give, give, give our love to others.

When you receive, remember that the Eucharist is the radiant fullness of God himself. That Jesus is entering you completely. That he is giving himself to you generously. That he is strengthening, transforming, and transfiguring you. That he is arming you with his presence, so that wherever you go you will radiate God to all you meet. That you will radiate God sometimes in silence, in hiddenness, and sometimes with words of consolation, encouragement, and hope to those whose faith has dimmed.

Go to every Eucharist like it was your first and your last. Go with a faithful expectancy that God's healing power, which is the strength of his own presence, will enter you.

Before going to Mass, pray for this faith. Pray to believe the words of the Mass in the deep recesses of your heart. Fold them within the wings of your intellect. Take those words into your heart every day. Let them feed you, move through you, restore you. Quietly and prayerfully ask for the grace to live the Mass.

Take that grace through the rest of the day and night. And again on each morrow receive the Word, the presence of the Lord himself. The Mass cannot be grasped with our minds. It is an incarnational reality. It weds each of us to the heart of the Trinity. It does so beyond and above anything we can understand.

The greatest sacramental is the human person. When we go to the Liturgy and receive the true presence of our Lord and Savior Jesus Christ, we walk away with his awesome presence throbbing in us and through us.

As we go about our daily tasks we must remember that it is our Lord's hand touching what we touch. It is the presence of the Lord in you and me that fleshes out our daily lives. It is the presence of the Lord speaking in us and through us if we so believe.

That is why we are constantly asking for the grace of faith. That is why we are constantly begging God to enlarge our heart. It's not to feel good, but to allow his love to fill every single corner of our mind, our heart, and our physical being.

Jesus lives in us through faith. Let's exercise this faith, exercise this belief and know that we are called as never before in the history of the world to counteract the terrible destructive forces through the love that flows out of us in our daily life.

The action lies in the inns of our hearts, for love is all that will last— the love we extend now and in the future. Love is the one thing that can never be destroyed. God lives and dwells in us, and he has ordained that love.

Your brothers and your sisters are the face of Christ.

Jesus Christ lives in each one of us. He feeds us with his Body and Word daily. We have nothing to do but to rest in his cradle of peace and let him continue to bring forth the impossible through his love.

God is in a hurry! The collapse of Western civilization is all around us. We are called to stand still in the midst of chaos, violence, and disorder, as we build a house of love for others in our hearts. The walls inside our hearts are breaking down. The restoration is speeding up within us.

"Be still, and know that I am God."[2]

Love is the only reality. We have dedicated and consecrated ourselves to gospel love, not human love. This is what our lives are meant to incarnate.

Our primary charism is to love God passionately, and to love and accept ourselves according to our God-given uniqueness. Then we can love one another. Never has it been more important that others touch the reality of God living in, with, and through each of us.

This begins at Mass.

God is present to us in this moment. Yesterday is gone, tomorrow has not come, all that we have is this present moment.

By accepting the duty of the moment and letting it guide us, we discover that this isn't our work, it's God's work.

2. Psalm 46:10 (NIV)

It is not the work that we do,
   but exercising our cocreative powers
      as members of the Mystical Body
         that uplifts and makes each day new.
It is not what we do that matters,
   but what God does in us and through us
      that matters and lasts.
That love can never be destroyed.
Believe, trust, and know
   that your daily life is of infinite importance
      to the kingdom of God.

Catherine's words ring in my ears, "Remember, I am only a voice!" She was God's conduit in ways we have only begun to grasp.

The Father hungers only to fill us with himself. He wants us to be poor, so as to be rich. To be chaste, so as to be pure. To be obedient, so as to return to the fullness of his love—love that comes to us through his daughter, Mary, Our Lady of Combermere.

The flame of the Holy Spirit hovers over each of us. Each moment our duty is to let it enflame us until there is nothing left but God. Such is our legacy. Such is our destiny. *Claim it!*

Our great work is really death to self.

A Way of the Cross

*Mary said, "You see before you the Lord's
servant, let it happen to me as you have said."
And the angel left her.*

— Luke 1:38

O Lord,
What little I have to give you—
you who gave everything
so that I could know you
and love you
and serve you.
Please, take me into your heart
and consume me
with the fire of your love.
I accept both joy and pain
as my constant companions
until I see you face to face.

The Liturgy is work. I recall that one day when the Liturgy began, we were all tired and out of sorts and in no "mood" to really take part in this work of love. Then during the Liturgy, somehow we were all caught up in the prayers in an unexpected and mysterious way. All of us felt and experienced the same energy filling us. When the priest was leaving after the last blessing, I looked at his face. It was absolutely radiant with a supernatural light.

Amid multiplying tensions in our life, this memory flitted in and out of my mind. The painful feelings and experiences we cause each other to have—the pain of the cross—is absolutely unavoidable, especially when we live so closely. I turn to our Lord saying, "What grace are you giving us at this time when we are so needy?"

This morning, I asked of Catherine, "You are our mother in the faith. Give me a hint as to what's transpiring." I waited. Nothing happened. Without thinking, I picked up the book *Poustinia*, opened it, and began reading:

"To reach the beatific vision, you must reach union with each other. In forming a family, a community of love, you have to accept the cross—embrace it gloriously and willingly. Your cross is composed of little things and of the acceptance of each other as you are. You must develop the ability to see the positive in each other, to see each other's beauty, to see each other's talents and to rejoice in them and be glad about them.

"As you grow in love, you help each other gently, peacefully, constantly, accepting the weaknesses of each other with deep love and great patience. That is how the Lord has treated you. Your first goal, which alone will lead you to the final goal, will be to establish a family, a community of love, accepting all the pain, the problems, the difficulty that every family must go through if it is going to be a community of love."[1]

This brought peace to my heart. Everyone was vulnerable, carrying some fatigue, and being stretched. That's what this tension was about.

Gradually, gently, the Eucharist penetrates the pain we carry in our inner beings. It may be our own pain, our neighbor's pain, or even the pain of someone in Sudan, India, or the parched, arid land of California. We don't know. It doesn't matter. What's important is that through our joy and pain we see that we are one with Jesus Christ, because he is one with all humanity.

This is our life. This is how he heals us of our sin and wounding. He only asks us to trust him more, and to accept everything with childlike faith and sureness that our pain will be transformed into good.

1. Catherine Doherty, "Poustinia in the Marketplace." In *Poustinia: Encountering God in Silence, Solitude and Prayer*. 3rd ed. (Combermere ON: Madonna House Publications, 2000), 63.

We're learning to do this as a family. We're beginning to see that we cannot live in the isolation of our own kingdoms. Our baptism unified us with Jesus, as does every Eucharist, every blessing, and every sacramental. The word of Scripture keeps bringing us back into the crucible of transforming divine love.

And so I say to those of us who are weary, stand straight and ask for relief from the living waters.

I beg God to infuse us with praise and gratitude, and ongoing prayer of the heart. These will join us to the suffering of other people throughout the world and transform the little things of daily life into opportunities for glorious atonement. In this way we can still carry the suffering of others even when we're unable to do so directly, physically, personally.

When one of us suffers, all of us suffer. When one of us is in joy, all of us are in joy. To embrace the personal crosses that come to us, we must discover within us the fullness of surrender that God alone can reveal.

We all loathe pain and suffering. It goes against our natural life-preserving instinct. But as we enter into the heart of suffering, we begin to realize that there can never be a life of God flourishing within us, consuming us—without suffering.

Back in the '70s, I remember walking into Catherine's cabin with Louise. She stopped, put her hands on her hips and said to Catherine, "I hate that plaque." The plaque she was referring to said "Pain is the Kiss of Christ."

During the Cana sessions, when families would gather there, it was not uncommon for parents to turn to that same plaque and make a remark about how often in the past year Christ had kissed them. They had the same natural aversion to pain that we all experience.

In her genius, Catherine knew that the power of pain is transformed when we offer it as a gift to the lover of mankind, Jesus Christ. That doesn't mean that we seek pain. But when it comes and when it's deep and long-lasting, something indescribable and grace-filled happens through the union of our pain with the cross of Jesus Christ.

Catherine carried an extraordinary amount of pain throughout her adult life. She plummeted its depths. She was victimized by revolution and war, which left her forever a stranger in a strange land. She constantly suffered rejection, abandonment, failure, and misunderstanding. The persecutions she suffered from priests alone, would have stretched most people's capacity to persevere. She endured

Jesus Christ ...
stay with us
through your
cross. . . .
We ask you to stay with the
Church; to stay with
humanity . . . Stay with us
in this deep mystery of your
death, in which you revealed
how much "God loved the
world." Stay with us and
draw us to yourself . . .
Stay with us through your
Mother, to whom, from the
cross, you specially entrusted
every human being. Stay
with us!

— John Paul II,
"Stay with us, Lord,
through your Cross"

because of her extraordinary love of Jesus Christ that began when she was a child.

We are all victims of our present civilization. Our civilization is very fragmented and brutally minimalizes Christ's incarnating mystery. Like Catherine, we too are called in some small way to help restore the Church. When we face our inevitable pain, we must remind ourselves that it is neither wasted, nor unnecessary.

The deep mystery of our life involves trusting, and unifying our pain with Jesus Christ, who is the absolute victor in this realm.

I second these words of Father Briere:

"Jesus calls us to a great love affair with him, but it must pass through the cross. Pain is the kiss of Christ, because the cross is the marriage bed of our spiritual espousal with Christ. Since suffering goes contrary to our nature, we tend to try to eliminate it from our lives. We must look at the reality of our Lord Jesus Christ.

"If we focus on him and his beloved face, our hearts will be touched by the Holy Spirit. We will yearn for greater and greater intimacy with him and with the Father and the Holy Spirit. We will yearn for this intimacy with the greatest awareness, with the consoling hand of Mary on our shoulders, and under the guidance and protection of St. Joseph.

"It's really all for love, isn't it? Desiring God's will and doing it the best we can, is the sure way to joy. Doing our own will is the surest and quickest way to self-destruction."

Pain is the kiss of Christ. Pain is the purifying fire of the Holy Spirit, working night and day to remove our false selves. Do not try to assuage this pain, to escape from it, or to be distracted from it.

If this world is to be restored to God, it needs a little army of people who don't count the cost, who willingly walk with God in trust and confidence, who willingly are stripped of what they possess for the glory of God and for the salvation of souls.

> Christians will often have to walk alone amidst uncomprehending crowds. They will have to be ready to be not only ridiculed but rejected with contempt.
>
> — Catherine Doherty

The Holocaust did not disappear when Hitler's genocidal attack on the Jews ceased. Forms of holocaust still stretch their tentacles around the globe due to today's culture of death. Divorce, suicide, abortion, euthanasia, hunger, poverty are monstrously growing forms of the destruction of human life and what it was created for.

Everyone can see the pressing decay of our civilization. Yet by taking our baptismal promise to God seriously, we become a sign of contradiction. You can be sure that we will be walking into a growing darkness. But the light of Jesus will be working in us and through us.

Being a sign of contradiction requires enormous faith. Trying to grasp what God is doing in us moment to moment, day by day, baffles and frustrates many people. Fortunately, hope is awakening within Christians all across the world. It's seeping under our doors, strengthening us, giving us more courage to love without counting the cost.

We must pray for priests and reverence the gift of the priesthood. Today they are experiencing heroic martyrdom (even if it is a white martyrdom) for the restoration of the many, many people who cry out for sanctification. They can only lead us if we pray for them.

Only in heaven is it known how some are called to lay down their lives for others in a special way. In silence and hiddenness, many have consecrated their entire lives as a sacrifice for priests. Doing this for priests, in this era, will bring about the salvation of many, many souls. For only priests bring us Jesus through the sacramental life, in a way that we will never completely understand until we are in heaven.

Jesus Christ is the one who established the Church, before the breakup of East and West, before its terrible splintering by the Protestant Reformation into so many different churches. Let's get our inner life, our prayer, and our daily life so focused on Jesus Christ that we will become a great vessel of love to help reunite and restore the Church, to help bring about the unity which our Lord has desired throughout history.

Love is the answer for the Church. The whole world suffers from the divisions that have taken place historically through the centuries. The body of Christ becomes more and more splintered as new denominations and new churches are established in the name of Christ. That is the agony of the body of Christ all over the world.

We who are little, unimportant, unseen, unheralded, and inconsequential, have been asked to incarnate the restoration of the body of Christ. Don't ever think that your part in this, even if it remains hidden for your entire life, is insignificant. What goes on in your heart has cosmic and eternal effects. Pray, fast, do penance, and cleanse your heart. Pray for the unity of all Christians.

God is at work in us, and the Accuser is working overtime trying to undermine everything God is doing in us.

We are sinners. That is a real part of our inner being that must be transformed. Since we're sinners, we must go through the flagellation and the mortification, the penance, the fasting, and the discipline of our ascetical exercises prescribed by the Church, especially during Lent. This will help us to become more tender, gentle, patient, loving, and receptive to the gospel of Jesus Christ. The Church realizes that without these, we'll become blobs on the face of the earth. But it's not these disciplines and mortifications that are the center of this work. We say, "I'm wounded" or "I can't help that because I'm wounded." We must learn to say, "No, it's not my wound that makes me mean and irritable and devious and hateful. It's the fact that I'm a sinner." But we are saved sinners, reaching up night and day for the mercy of God.

When God is at work in your heart, you are likely to be tempted to declare, "I have this right, or I need this or that." Extinguish these subtle temptations by asking yourself, "Do I need it? Or do I want it?" Ask yourself, "Does it give me status, security, and affirmation?" If so, perhaps you are looking for the right kind of life in the wrong kind of places. Ask, "Is it the outside of the cup that needs cleansing or the inside?"

Dying to everything except the Jesus Christ who lives in our own flesh is the beginning. It gives us only momentary relief, though. It's not all that God asks of us. There is so much more.

Jesus Christ is bleeding again. He is being crucified once more in his Church. Will you love this Jesus in his mystical body? Will you wipe away his tears and his Mother's tears with your hidden surrender to him? Are you willing to help him bring forth again that which we all desire?

> *How few know what true love is.*
> *How few see the dancing flames of joy in the somber ashes of pain.*
>
> — Catherine Doherty

Each one of us must go deeply into our lives, into the spiritual heritage that the Church has placed in our hands. Only by living what God has given us, will his work be accomplished in and through us.

I beg you to stop blaming, criticizing, and tearing one another apart with human rationalizations and emotional woundings. Claim your own pain. Take it to the foot of the cross. Look up and let Jesus heal you.

The pain of daily rubbing up against one another resolves itself only by taking our burdens to the foot of the cross, by forgiving, and by trusting that Jesus will restore us.

To carry the cross of our brother or sister requires grace. Let's be sure that we're given that grace before we take up what our legs may be too wobbly to carry. For this we need spiritual directors. Obedience to a spiritual director helps us to stay faithful and to discern what restoration of the Church will come through each of us.

We must do everything in our power to shed our lies and false burdens that come from our selfishness and neuroses. Then we will glory in every little thing that God sends us. We then progress step by step. Together let's stay close to our spiritual directors, close to our elders, so that hand in hand we can embrace the great calling in life that Jesus Christ has given to us. Our Lady will be our guide and anchor.

The most crucial focus for offering our lives for one another is *sobornost*. By dying to our selfishness, our unity of mind and heart is made a living reality. Here lies the secret of peace and concord between men and women, parents and children, East and West, North and South, rich and poor, abused and abuser. Nothing will stop God's Word from reaching his full stature in us, when we allow him to love us, and when we love him and one another in return.

Our cross is very simple. We put one hand in the hand of Jesus and the other hand in the hand of our neighbor. We can walk hand in hand with courage and total confidence that our faith will bring us more hope with each passing day, and that love will be an explosion, a holocaust, a shining reality, because we who are little have trusted him who is great.

We have joined in a communal consecration to Our Lady. Trust and stand in the joy of the cross, so that all of us can be a bonfire of love for this world, which seems to be hovering on the abyss of destruction. Once we have surrendered to our pain, there is nothing that will stop the joy of the Lord's presence in us from moving outward to every corner of the earth.

Remember your consecration. Our sorrow, our struggle, our humanity can and will be lifted up as we chew on the truth of the gospel. All of us must go through the agony in the garden and walk the *Via Dolorosa* to be glorified through God's mercy. There is no other way. Let's walk hand in hand into that glory quickly, for the salvation of souls.

These words of Father Pelton, written years ago, are more valid today than ever: "We are being asked by Christ to show the infinite humility of his heart, the tenderness of his Mother, and the impossible unity that only the grace of the cross can achieve."

Everyone who touches us suffers in the same way that we suffer, because we are suffering with Jesus Christ. We are challenging today's modern world..

We must be armed with joy and incredible shining faith and love knowing that we live in Christ and Christ lives in us. You who are discouraged, can you not place on the altar that discouragement, for those who are suffering all over the world?

You who are in fear, can you not lay that fear at the foot of the cross or take it to Mass? In this way your fear can bear fruit to the far corners of the earth, for those who are hungry and homeless and do not know God.

You who suffer tension between yourself and another person, will you not give this in silence and hiddenness to Jesus, so that new life and new hope can be born again for someone in need?

When we consecrate ourselves, we, in some mysterious way, become deeply united with the whole church, with the entire body of Christ throughout the world. In the West, we are prone to look only at our individual suffering. But, bit by bit, the veils to truth are falling from our eyes. We're beginning to see that there is something far beyond ourselves as individuals that is taking place in the world. I'm hearing again some expressions that were once more common: "remain united to the cross," "offer it up for the sufferings of Christ." This indicates that people are seeing more clearly again, seeing with the eyes of the gospel.

Everyone hates pain. Pain in and of itself is an evil. But no one can escape it. All of us are caught up in its mystery. If we want to be emptied, transformed, and divinized, we must, through an act of our will, unite our pain with the sufferings of Jesus Christ. Then our pain becomes a gift, and grace flows from this gift and does something powerful and mysterious in the depths of our souls.

Christ . . . said very clearly: "If any man would come after me . . . let him take up his cross daily." . . . Suffering is, in itself, an experience of evil. But Christ has made suffering the firmest basis of the definitive good. . . of eternal salvation. . . . In that "cosmic" struggle between the spiritual powers of good and evil . . . human sufferings, united to the redemptive suffering of Christ, constitute a special support for the powers of good, and open the way to the victory of these salvific powers.

— John Paul II,
Salvifici Doloris

*W*e avoid pain at all costs; on a human level we try to escape this affliction. But there is a pain that brings great joy. It is perhaps the greatest call of love that can be offered to us. It is an invitation that comes from Jesus Christ to offer our lives in union with his passion, death and resurrection for all of our brothers and sisters throughout the world. It is his Mother who shows us how to accept this invitation.

*W*e are celebrating the anniversary of Nuje's death. All of Nuje's life was a mystery that only God could penetrate. Physically, mentally, and psychologically she bore wounds that undeniably scare this century. One of her great sorrows was that she always felt she never measured up to what she thought was "a good staff worker." She failed royally in what we project on one another in our shallow judgments and criticisms. But anyone who knew Nuje never failed to experience the warm bath of tenderness and compassion that poured out of her—if you had the courage to open your heart to her. I never left her room without experiencing an overwhelming sense of peace in my heart and soul.

Sometime in the '80s, Nuje asked what I thought of her becoming a victim soul.[2] She pursued this on the feast of the Transfiguration in 1987. After her death, the prayer she wrote to make her offering came to my attention. These are some excerpts from her prayer:

"Most Holy and Triune God, Father, Son and Holy Spirit, through the Sacred Heart of Jesus and the Immaculate Heart of Mary, Theotokos, and often hidden Mother of my life and faith, I wish to offer to you my life as a victim soul.

"Please, in your mercy, accept my total being as a suffering servant; in atonement for my own flawed and sinful life, and especially for this world gone mad, and your children in it who are prey to every temptation and life-sapping heresy. I surrender myself into your still, bottomless, loving heart, Christ Jesus. I beg you to be my all in all, in my life of ordinariness. God alone!

"Please, let me offer my share in your sufferings for priests, your own chosen ones, especially your vicar, the pope, the bishops and all who carry out your priesthood from the least to the greatest. . . .

"Please accept this life in gratitude for the gift of faith and this vocation. Take the life itself, now, if you wish, or day by day in longevity. Both, at one time or another have been loved and feared. Thy will be done.

---

2. One who offers their life with all its sufferings and joys to the Father in imitation of Jesus on Calvary and in atonement for sins, and for the salvation of souls. This indicates a radical affirmation of our baptismal promises.

"Let me be a sign of your incredible mercy and healing for all the 'weak like me' people; let your wounds be shown and touched in your 'April Fool.'[3]

"I beg, sure of a hearing, for three things: An open, listening heart and ear; Tears to 'water the stick' and weep for those, who in their pain cannot, and for joy in your mercy; Gratitude for your life, death, and resurrection, and your great mercy.

"As a slave of Mary, everything is in her hands, your hands.

"Lord Jesus Christ, Son of the living God, have mercy on me, a sinner. Jesus, I love you.

"Signed, Ray Gene."

Catherine said that only after we have completed our crucifixion, one by one, will we enter our Nazareth. One by one, the unstoppable cosmic radiation of love grows and grows in the heart of the Church. Our personal transformation through the cross allows us to incarnate Christ in the world. That's why we must embrace all of our pain with joy, confidence, and surrender.

No one can escape radical crucifixion, because it is given to us by God himself, to empty us so he can fill us with himself.

We are being stretched. We are being stretched by love, from one end of the world to the other. If you see with eyes of faith, you see that as the world situation continues to crescendo into some kind of confrontation, the living presence of God is asking us to come closer to him. We're more

3. Ray Gene (a member of Madonna House also known lovingly as Nuje) was born on April 1st.

and more conscious that we do this mainly by standing still interiorly. That is why our unity is so crucial these days, for our unity is found in the mind and the heart of Jesus Christ.

The tragedy of not dying to our false self is that we never grow into the full stature that God intended.

We are becoming God's fiery furnace, prepared for love by pain. We are buffeted by temptations and doubts, pulled in all directions, tempted to get off the path that leads us into the love of God. Perseverance comes only through prayer. Even when everything around us pulls us away from God's love, we must hunger for it, pray for it, and most of all stand still in it.

Little Acts of Love

And Mary said:
"My soul proclaims the greatness of the Lord
and my spirit rejoices in God my Savior."

— Luke 1:46–47

Let us join hands and pray this prayer from Catherine's heart:

"Lord, behold,

We are all kneeling here together,

Asking you to give us an increase of faith.

Let our hearts be open to you.

Let our heads be put into our hearts.

Let faith, hope, love, trust, and confidence reign among us.

Let us be done with human respect.

Let us be done with being afraid of ridicule.

Let us be done with thinking we have to hide anything

    from one another.

Lord behold,

We are in need of healing."[1]

Hunger for the contemplative life has grown inside each of us. We all have a glorious, soothing, and cool image of having heaven on earth, and we hunger and desire to be one with the Blessed Trinity. But to be a contemplative and to live the "poustinia of the heart" in the midst of our daily marketplace is the greatest challenge we have as sons and daughters of Catherine.

This is our life. It was also the life of Our Lady and her Son in Nazareth. They lived the ordinary daily life of the people around them while holding, hidden, this gold of divinity that has become our heritage as well.

To remind us of what our daily interior life is to be, wherever we are, I've gleaned from Catherine's words these kernels for living the poustinia of the heart:

1. Doherty, "Touching God." In *Poustinia*, 130.

"When I was thrown into the noisiest marketplaces in the world, God showed me how to live out the poustinia. . . . The essence of the poustinia is that it is a place within one's self, a result of baptism, where each of us contemplates the Trinity. . . . It's as if I were sitting next to God in complete silence, although there are many other people around.

"The poustinik enters his poustinia and takes humanity with him . . . with all its pain, sorrows, joys, everything. . . . He becomes the minority group, the poor, the restless rich. He is everyone.

"By his inner solitude . . . he becomes one with God, who became man. . . . In identifying with Christ . . . I can love and identify with others. . . . By listening to the great silence of God and having this strange, passive dialogue . . . I become aware of the silence which is the speech of God. . . . It is only by listening to this silence that I can acquire a listening heart. . . . The poustinia is walking this inner solitude, immersed in the silence of God. My life of service and love to my fellow man is simply the echo of this silence and solitude.

"I am immersed in the Trinity and the fire of the silence of God. I become as one on fire with love of him. . . . When my immersion into this silence has finally caught fire, then I am able to speak. . .because his voice is sounding loudly and clearly in my ears which have been emptied of everything except him.

"Now only his name is on my heart. It has become my heartbeat.

"In order to form a community of love with men, we must make contact with the Trinity, the original community of love. . . . We must begin by emptying ourselves of all our goods and going forth into the solitude and immense silence of God. . . . When you have given up your silver, your gold, your parents, your friends, then you enter into the physical solitude, but you still take with you the I that is me, this selfish I. In this inner poustinia, you must now empty yourself."[2]

The moment graces come, we must always be alert and watchful. You can be sure that the enemy lurks in the shadows, doing everything possible to make us sluggish, complacent, and divided. Each one of us must go into the inn of our hearts and do violence to the negative forces lurking in hidden chambers of our minds and hearts.

We must pray daily for the grace to love, to serve, and to take the last place in all things. Humility and simplicity come only when we trust and allow God to do what he wants with each of us.

Never fear pain! Ninety-nine chances out of a hundred, whatever pain you may be carrying at this moment has nothing to do with your own stubborn heart, but is a gift of love for someone who does not have the multitudinous blessings that come to us each day. Do you realize we are blessed more times than we can count in a day? We have access to Confession. We receive the Eucharist daily.

We suffer in this age because of divisions. We suffer in this age because of unforgiveness and self-centeredness. We who live the Christian life must see with new eyes and hear with restored ears, so that we can see and hear every little thing in everyday life as salvific. Pope John Paul II has pushed against this tidal wave of history that has blocked everyone from receiving the splendor that the universal church can give.

2. Doherty, "The Poustinia of the Heart." In *Poustinia*, 183–187.

Your eyes and ears and heart must be recreated daily through repentance and conversion. Never think that you've arrived. Never think that the Lord is finished with you.

Until the whole earth is filled with the glory of God, we have to be available and compliant to his desire to reveal his glory, person to person, in unique and bold ways.

Never get stuck in a narrow vision. Keep your eyes wide open and learn from everyone. Every person who comes to you is a presence of God. Ask yourself, "What will this person teach me?" And not only, "What can I give?" but, "What can I receive?" As we give and receive, we will be enriched. Our cup will overflow, our hearts will expand, and love will grow.

Let us wash our faces and be radiant as we pray and fast, atone and get cleansed for the great moment of the Resurrection.

Yes was the silent *fiat* of the Mother of God which transformed and made possible the re-creation of the kingdom of God on earth. Let us ponder deeply the ultimate power of saying that one little word as we join her *fiat* day by day.

There is a heavenly plan. It is not our gifts or talents, and certainly not our intellect, that will bring forth what God has planned for us. It will only come forth from a spirit of poverty, chastity, and obedience. We cannot live in God's plan without a profound and deep surrender in faith to everything asked of us day by day.

Lay aside everything that was important yesterday. Human means will be limited in the days ahead. We must climb the mountain of the Lord and rejoice in praise and exultation for everything that comes our way. Every pain will turn into joy as long as we give thanks, honor, and glory to God every minute of every day.

We have the grace we need to correct what we know needs to be corrected within ourselves. The rest is placing ourselves completely in the hands of God and laying the mantle of love, mercy, and tenderness over one another.

I bow low before the Trinity, and I bow low with gratitude to each of you who in silence have rendered a *fiat* to whatever the Lord asks each day.

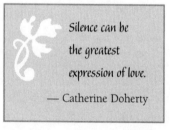

Silence can be the greatest expression of love.

— Catherine Doherty

The earthly lives of Jesus and Mary and Joseph seemed little, humble, ordinary, and hidden, but they've had a cosmic and eternal effect. So too, your little, humble, and hidden daily life has a cosmic effect upon this world staggering under problems far beyond any human solution.

In little ways each day, we die to our selfishness, greed, and desires for attention and control, so that Christ can live in us. Each day we consume Christ's Body at the Eucharist, which feeds millions who do not know him, as we faithfully do the little things asked of us.

We use the word "Nazareth" over and over again. What does it mean in this period of the Church? It means beginning again. Our Lord is asking us to live the gospel life in a new way and yet in a very old way. All of us have lost the true light and direction that brings forth this new creation. We struggle with our wounds and sinfulness. Do not fear. Our Lord gave us to his Mother.

Your hidden, humble, ordinary life is important to the Lord Jesus Christ. We're at a point in history where we have to take up the sling like David in the Old Testament and slay this culture of death through the power of fulfilling our "duty of the moment" as little people and through love.

We have absolutely nothing to fear. We have only to surrender and walk without wavering in fidelity to the duty of the moment that each one of us meets on this day.

I believe that all of us here are beginning to clearly see how vital it is to simply do the duty of the moment. No gathering of politicians, no council for ecumenism, no human being can turn this massive battle around, only heaven. Over the past two or three years, our Lord and Our Lady have given us the grace to collectively enter more deeply into conversion, repentance, and inner freedom, not just for ourselves but for the whole world.

In our little corner of Canada, under the protection of Our Lady of Combermere, we seem to be the least, the most forgotten of the new lay communities. But if you meditate on heaven's promise to bring to fulfillment the spiritual inheritance given to us through Catherine, you begin to comprehend what God is doing in each of us. It's only through incarnation that the restoration of the world and the restoration of our Christian heritage takes place. Be bold! Trust God as never before! Let's ask for everything that we need.

> The secret of daily living is to connect an ordinary, seemingly boring life, with all its repetitive details, with Love who is God.
>
> — Catherine Doherty

We must grasp the height and depth of the ordinariness, the hiddenness, and the grandeur of doing little things well for the love of God.

This is a time of grave crisis. The essential problem in every nation is a spiritual one. We, who have been called, cannot do big things. But we all can give the love we are given this day to anyone who comes to us. We can pray for the grace to be purified, so that we can help carry one another's burdens with gentleness, understanding, and compassion.

We must move. We must open up the doors of our homes and our hearts. We must grow in faith, so that love can come to every cell in our bodies, so that we can pass on to those who come through our doors the presence of Jesus Christ, the presence of his Mother, the presence of Love incarnated in and through us.

A new page is being written in our lives, and it begins by plunging into the heart of faith. Only through faith can we hear or see or speak. A hand will touch our ears and they will be open, not only to human words but to God's words. A hand will touch our eyes and we will see with the eyes of God. A hand will touch our tongues and we will speak, not as men do but as God speaks.

Bowing of our being to God and to one another has to increase. This is a house of love, and the great need today is for what only love can bring, love who is God. Heroic and great and small steps are being taken everywhere, so that unity of mind and heart will become incarnated, in spite of multiple difficulties.

We have been handed something that goes far beyond what can be achieved on a natural level. We're all aware of that, but we must trust that what God wants, God will have. The questions for all of us together and in our personal journeys to the heart of God are, "Am I listening? Am I receiving? Am I absorbing? Am I giving to others what has been given to me?"

The old spiritual law of the saints is: The more you give, the more you receive; the more you love, the more you are loved.

The trick is not to have a hidden agenda while giving and loving, though, in which a subtle but real expectation serves as your ulterior motive. We look to our Savior, rather than those we love, to fulfill us. Only Jesus Christ can give you and me what we give away.

Only when you and I depend on our Lord and Savior Jesus Christ every minute of every day can we become a hymn of love. If you have a snag in the journey, then somewhere you are making a mistake and putting expectations on someone or something.

At the heart of this work of God is sanctifying, humble, ordinary everyday work. We wrap ourselves in repetitive daily tasks rooted close to the earth, doing work that typical moderns would call unsatisfying. We're to be little as was Our Lady, to be hidden as were Jesus, Mary, and Joseph, and to allow God to love us for others.

Lay people are the leaven and the dough. We need fervent dedicated lay people to bring about the revolution of love in modern society that's waiting for us. We enter the marketplace and begin the transformation of society into the gospel pattern. We can't do it all ourselves, but we touch many people in our houses and influence them in ways we can hardly imagine. We need to be reminded of how connections are made in our daily lives. Reflect again and again on this quiet incarnational life.

> *Workers are invited to unite themselves with the Savior's work. As the Council says: "Indeed by their active charity, rejoicing in hope, and bearing one another's burdens, they imitate Christ, who worked as a carpenter and is always working with the Father for the salvation of all." Thus the salvific value of work . . . is revealed at a very high level as a sharing in the sublime work of Redemption.*
>
> — John Paul II,
> *Lay Work Shares
> in Christ's Mission*

Anyone who is loving and serving is not only on the path to God, but is an instrument for his marvelous fire of love to pass through. This is not an emotional love. It is the hidden, mysterious force of God moving through his creature, transmitting grace to others.

Each of us is called to make radical, deep, and eternal choices, minute by minute, day by day.

Do you love everyone who comes to you, without judgment? To do this we must feed ourselves on the gospel of Jesus Christ, letting it enter our being. We must pray always, in the secret chambers of our heart.

We must reverence and respect one another. We're all at different levels. Each is being fed by the many streams of our heritage.

Up until now, we've had a great need to remove the blocks, barriers, and resistance in our minds and psyches, caused by wounding and sin. This process will continue until the day we die. But at least we have the wherewithal to still stand before God and claim our own life.

This is sound advice given us by Father Briere:

We are meant to live in harmony, compassion, tenderness, and mercy.

We are meant to live with one mind and one heart, so that we can be a presence of love and truth for all who come to us at this time in the history of the world, seeking food for their starving souls and spirits.

The great need today is for people to be fed with our spiritual treasures. We have these treasures in our heritage but they will not expand or multiply unless we give them to all who come to us, and especially to those we live with right at this moment.

When you are up against any resistance, negativity, hardness of heart, any blocks within yourself or in your brother or sister pray quietly and repetitively until you feel that resistance or negativity lift from you.

Let's make a resolution to be gentle with one another, to speak words that build one another's confidence and trust, to see only what is godly in one another, and to guard our thoughts against accusations that can tear the bleeding body of Jesus Christ. We are restorers of life, first within our own hearts, then with one another, and then for the whole world. I pray that this year we each decrease, and that the presence of the humble and majestic Christ grows in each of us through the power of the sanctifying Holy Spirit.

Let us pray for one another and keep the door of our hearts open to receive more and more life. Let no one be afraid, for God is melting, through the power of the Incarnation, the fear that is in all of us.

Nothing can overcome you. Let God dwell in you, move in you. Let him consume you. He alone is trustworthy. He is the only one who will never hurt or disappoint you. Embrace every minute of every day with childlike trust, and pray for faith and more faith.

We can meet the difficulties that lay ahead through loving one another. We will definitely be a bulwark against the darkness. And grace will be sent across the earth through the Mother of God to her children who need the spirit that comes from our consecrated life and our love.

Life is short. Our most important focus from now until we see God face to face is to be consumed by love in order to love. All things in the world fade, but love is eternal.

Let us pray that we can walk hand in hand, being patient as we love one another, never judging, never criticizing, never blaming our brothers and sisters, but praying that we can have the crown of white martyrdom. We must prepare. Its crowning will come in God's timetable for each of us.

The Holy Spirit is fire and light. He enters the depths of our souls, penetrates the deepest recesses of our being, and becomes a permanent guest there. He is the artist of souls, the Sanctifier, the purifier, the Advocate, and ultimately is given to us to bring forth the fullness and perfect possession of love.

We all know that at baptism we are welded to Jesus and receive all the gifts of the Spirit. God loves us through the Holy Spirit. No act of love can be in us without the action of the Holy Spirit. It is the Holy Spirit who breaks open the Word. His creative power brings forth in us the unique image and likeness that God the Father had in his mind and heart always.

Every Christian is redeemed by Jesus Christ.

As Archbishop Raya said, "*Live. Be free.*"

We must believe in our Baptism.

We must believe in the Eucharist.

We must believe in the forgiveness of our sins, not because of what we do, but because we have a Savior who is not only a good God, but a God who has already done for us what is necessary to restore us to being creatures of extraordinary peace and love, who radiate the Trinity from our hearts, our souls and our spirits.

Each of us has to do violence to ourselves, in order to expand that place inside of us where God lives and desires to be more fully present every day. The stripping, emptying, and trust in the Trinity dwelling within us will be different for each of us.

We will become a word of liquid gold that will flow across not only Canada but the whole world, if we can throw ourselves at the feet of the Lord and say, "Do what you will with me. I trust you! I trust you!" If we can accept whatever happens to us as it comes through people, events, and situations in the ordinary, everyday life of life; if we can trust and believe that the only path to the freedom we seek, and to the joy of the risen Lord in each one of us is through joy and pain. This life that has been placed in our hands through Catherine is pushing on all of us, and we must have courage and confidence to meet God in the inner chambers of our heart in silence and solitude. Do it today! Do it now!

Catherine said, time and time again, "You have to put your mind in your heart."

How many times a day do you stop to open your heart and simply ask God to fill you, love you, and dwell in you? How many times a day do you raise your mind and heart in faith to bless your brothers and sisters when they hurt you, when they judge you, when they speak unkindly about you? It is our faith that heals us. It is our faith, given to us in Baptism, that has to be exercised and become a hallmark of our primary relationship with the Father. Only then are we free to pass on that love as we go about the little things of our daily life.

Chapter VI

Confessing Humbly

*He has looked upon the humiliation
of his servant. Yes, from now onwards
all generations will call me blessed.*

— Luke 1:48

Give me fortitude,
please, I need your courage,
for I am weak and needy
at this moment.

The person you hurt the most when you are negative is yourself.

Our negativity upsets our own peace, fullness of life, and ability to love according to the gospel. We fall many times a day. That's not the issue. What's crucial is what we do with negativity and how quickly we can put it into perspective, through prayer, forgiveness, and leaving to God what is his business and not ours.

When this kind of disruption occurs between people, it's a sign that God is at work. We get blown into the crucible with one another, because we're putting our heart and might into doing something God desires.

Remind yourself again and again that your brother or sister is not the problem. We're up against powers and principalities. We have to learn how to contend with them.

We can find the truth in Scripture, and in the wisdom and tradition of the Church. The Church's members have always been sinful, imperfect, and weak, but the Church is the vessel created out of the side of Christ to sustain us and keep us in truth and love until our Lord returns again.

There's always someone praying for perseverance among us. We need this prayer, because the walk into eternity is arduous. To be shorn and cleansed of the things in us that are not divine is a painful process, but God will give us the grace we need to take one step at a time.

We only have one enemy—the master of deceit. Every person on earth belongs to God. Do not slander or judge anyone, even if the person robs, kills, or violates other people. Keep your focus on the Trinity and be faithful to your life of poverty, chastity, and obedience. God will correct the rest.

Emptying our minds and hearts each day of falsehood and lies allows us to become transformed by God.

Concern yourself only with the lies in your own heart, mind, and psyche. After those lies are brought to light, you'll be able to forgive everyone who has hurt you and enter into the truth of the gospel. There we can sing and dance with joy together.

The catastrophe on earth is not between people, but between God and the forces of darkness, between life and death, love and hate. Your brother and sister are not your enemy. The enemy is the interior voice that lies to you about yourself and others.

You cannot change another, but you can change yourself. Find your life in God first. Seek his kingdom in your own heart, and everything will come to you. You are the temple of the Holy Spirit, and the house of the Father and the Son, as well. *Call upon them often.*

The interior spiritual struggle is increasing. Ask Our Lady to lead you, form you, and give you faith, the faith that she had in her earthly life and offers for the entire Church. Seek help as you need it, but live with the confidence that each of us are indestructibly wrapped in God's heart.

The Church and her missionaries must also bear the witness of humility, above all with regard to themselves—a humility which allows them to make a personal and communal examination of conscience in order to correct in their behavior whatever is contrary to the gospel and disfigures the face of Christ.

— John Paul II, Redemptoris Missio

*W*e must always be careful when we speak of the errors that have come down through history. In no way does it follow that the bride of Christ, which is the Church, is anything but pure and unspotted. When we receive the sacramental life through the ordained priest, be it Baptism, Confirmation, the Eucharist, or healing, we know in faith that the purity of the life of Christ flows into our soul. Nothing can mar that, and the teaching Church remains unspotted when it comes to dogmas of our faith as the Holy Father proclaims them.

*O*pen the doors of repentance!

Open wide the doors of repentance, all you children of Our Lady of Combermere!

Open wide the gates of forgiveness!

Open wide the gates of your heart, so that we can be in the flood of grace that is coming from the universal Church!

What holds you back? Reflect on some of the things that taint the wellspring of love acquired through Baptism, Eucharist, and Confirmation.

Is your faith weak?

Are you judging others?

Do you fail to forgive, seventy times seven?

Do you distrust authority or one another?

Are you being a perfectionist?

Are you concerned about how you appear to others?

Are you racked with fear or spiritual rebellion?

Do you protect yourself?

Are you so laid back that you don't even make an effort?

Do you desire power?

Do you compare yourself to others?

Are you failing to listen to your brother and sister?

Perhaps instead of listening to the voice of truth, you've become accustomed to listening to the accuser or liar. Discern the messages you're listening to.

Do you think, "My situation will never get better?"

Do you chastise yourself and think, "I have to be perfect"?

Are you unmoored by feeling that you have to do something, rather than wanting to do something?

Do you ever think, "No one cares," "I don't matter," or "God doesn't take any interest in or care of me"?

Does a voice inside you say, "Those who are responsible for me, don't understand me," "No one will listen to me," or "No one cares what I have to say"?

Do you equate disagreement with disloyalty?

Do you ever think, "I'm not as good as so and so?"

In the morning, do you fall down to adore and praise God, or do you chase an idol?

Is it your desire to control?

Do you try to be first instead of last?

Are you consumed by shame?

Do fleshy urges distract you?

Are relationships, and being liked, admired, or preferred more important to you than loving, serving, and listening to the voice of the Holy Spirit?

All of us hear voices that come from within and without us. The voice of God is gentle and kind, merciful, slow to anger, full of patience. Read the Hymn of Love:

"Love is always patient and kind; love is never jealous; love is not boastful or conceited, it is never rude and never seeks its own advantage, it does not take offence or store up grievances. Love does not rejoice at wrongdoing, but finds its joy in the truth. It is always ready to make allowances, to trust, to hope, and to endure whatever comes. Love never comes to an end."[1]

Listen to that voice as it comes in one way or another, through the day. Feed your heart with thoughts from this great wealth of tenderness, compassion, mercy, and acceptance of others, just as they are.

1. 1 Corinthians 13:4–8

How many times have we heard, "With God, every moment is the moment of beginning again"? Every moment we must make a choice to live or die, to bless or curse. We have the potential within us to transmit the divine presence given to us through our baptism, or to crush, destroy, and put down ourselves, as well as our brothers and sisters. If today you hear his voice, harden not your heart.

> *We must realize the necessity of accepting our weaknesses and God's strength, and of showing them to the world.*
>
> — Catherine Doherty

Soak in the words that Archbishop Neil McNeil spoke to Catherine at the beginning of her apostolate. Catherine often reflected upon them:

"Catherine, I called to tell you, to beg you: *persevere*.

"If you do, your Apostolate will cover the world, but you must know, understand, realize now that you are going to suffer very much. I called you because I see your sufferings. The eyes of death approaching me make my sight clear.

"I have been praying much for you. I wanted to see you. You are the least of my flock. That is why I saw you first, even before my priests. I will pray for you before the face of God when I get there. But now I beg you, as the father of your soul, as you always called me, to *persevere*.

"The Church will need the lay apostolate in the decades to come, and you are pioneering it. God has specially called you. Now I will bless you for that perseverance."

Each of us are to go into the depths of our heart, to confront what separates us from our Lord and Savior, Jesus Christ—

being sinned against, sinning, not trusting, not believing, not realizing that we can do nothing without God.

Let us pray for the gift of perseverance. Let us pray that our hearts be open for God to move us and lead us on the paths that he clears for us to spread the gospel.

The laity, as part of the Church, are called to enter this great work. The priests feed us through the Sacraments, cover us with blessings, and open up avenues that lead us into the heart of the Church and humanity. But we have a grave responsibility to transmit this flood of love—the presence of God in us—to all who come to us. They come in order to be fed from our faith, love, and our humble little life, which was born from the love of God in order to bring peace to all who come to us.

All of us experience maternal and paternal wounding. Our wounding comes from the old creature. The new creature comes from gospel living and our vocation.

As an authority figure, I am unable to help in your step-by-step conversion from that wounding. The gospel says we cannot go back to our mother's womb. My grace for you lies in a different area, as your director general and as a mother to our family. Whenever I have been asked by you to heal these wounds, I have been powerless. My grace does not lie there.

But all of us need someone to help us with our wounding. This is a universal circumstance. When you ask me, I can love you, stand by you in your pain and give it to the crucified Lord, and pray for your rebirth in the Spirit. But you need to work through your wounding with someone who does not have a role of authority in your life, such as an elder, a counselor, or a psychiatrist.

Do not project feelings of fear, anger, rejection, or abandonment onto anyone else. This only increases the pain already being carried. Deflect your hurting to a safe place— to a person who has the tools and the grace to help you.

*O*ur hunger for love is universal. No one can fill our emptiness but God. We must learn to separate our childhood wounding from those circumstances causing us pain today.

Jean Vanier said, "We never get totally healed from our old wounds. We eventually learn to live around and through our wounds." Let the awareness of wounding be a source of tenderness, compassion, gentleness, and unity as we consider what another is going through.

*W*e come from a polluted world. We've all absorbed ideas and emotional battering that have wounded us beyond recognition. Underneath every wound is a sin. Please take this seriously. Our wounding is typically from childhood victimization. When we turn our face to God, we progressively have to face our woundedness and our pain, with all its shoots of negativity, and begin a profound repentance and conversion. Meditate on this passage from Hebrews:

"The word of God is something alive and active: it cuts more incisively than any two-edged sword: it can seek out the place where soul is divided from spirit, or joints from marrow; it can pass judgment on secret emotions and thoughts. No created thing is hidden from him; everything is uncovered and stretched fully open to the eyes of the one to whom we must give account of ourselves."[2]

We are being offered the gift of greater life. For many it is very painful, but the promise of Our Lady will come to fruition.

In essence, the light coming from the suffering of many people is quite simple. It is not what happens to you that matters but how you react to it. All of us have been hurt and all of us have a million hidden grievances from long ago buried in our minds and hearts. Who can say that they don't have resentment, bitterness, frustration, or an occasional burst of anger? Well, if you can honestly say, "I don't," then you are totally transformed and in a state of sanctification. Most of us are still struggling.

I urge each of you to go before the Lord in the sacrament of Penance. Ask for forgiveness of *all* of your sins—from childhood to the present. Confess all of the sins that you can recall through the help and light of the Holy Spirit.

When we repent of our personal sins, then, as pure instruments we will be able to fulfill our promises and our fidelity to the gospel, both as individuals and as a body. We are part and parcel of the greater Church. When one receives a grace, it has a rippling effect on all of us.

2. Hebrews 4:12–13

The glory of God is upon you. The Holy Spirit works deeply through your own joy and pain. Each of us needs to practice ongoing forgiveness and repentance. We especially need to repent of the chronic mental sins of *judging* and *resentment*.

The biggest block, though, is not believing that God loves every cell in our bodies. We need to pray that we can receive his love more and more. We must go to him like a beggar for the grace to receive his love and to stay open to the love of our brothers and sisters. Doing and giving are very meritorious, but the block God is uncovering is how little we embrace and believe in our heart and spirit that God loves us.

Fortunately, we have a good God who is patient, kind, merciful, tender, and constantly drawing us through all kinds of clues, events, and people back into his flaming heart of love.

What is the meaning of repentance? Essentially, repentance is such sorrow for sin or a fault that one is disposed to change one's life for the better.

It's typically taken to mean feeling sorrow for sin, a feeling of guilt, a sense of grief at wounds that have been inflicted on others and ourselves. But this meaning leaves out the most important part. The deeper understanding requires a change of mind, not just regret for the past. For the Christian, it is a fundamental transformation of our outlook on ourselves, others, and on God.

Metanoia requires total *kenosis* and change. East and West really take us to the same glory of God, but use different words in this transformation process. *Metanoia* is more akin to transformation of life or change of heart. Sorrow and grief are necessary prerequisites to change, and they open the door to a new way of looking at one's self, others, and God. But in

this movement the positive note of hope and healing is crucial, in order to be transported beyond sorrow and grief to a
life filled with the potential of God's grace.

Pray for your brothers and sisters. Pray that we confess and
put to rest under the Sacrament whatever sins still operate in
us, so that we won't be an obstacle to loving our brothers and
sisters as God wants us to love them.

The cross marking Catherine's grave reads simply, "She loved
the poor."

Indeed she did love the poor, not only the economic
poor but those who were forgotten, rejected, humiliated, and
cast off by society. She saw in them the image of God in a very
extraordinary way.

When God gathered us together and brought us into Our
Lady's house, we may have come thinking that we were
alright. But we soon discover that we are poor and sinful.

Part of the call to this Apostolate is peeling back the layers of our own poverty until we realize that we are the
Brother Christopher (the poor person on the street), we are
the prostitute, we are the least and the littlest. It's as though
God in his mercy and in his great love for us allows us to
identify little by little, and more and more as the years go by,
with everyone. Our love grows in proportion as we see all
those elements in our heart where we have rejected the beauty and dignity of our true self.

If Jesus came into the world as a poor man, why should we not rejoice in our poverty? Why should we not rejoice in our purity of heart that comes from giving back to God the power of our sexuality for his glory? He did this, and his Mother did it, so we're in good company. He was obedient even unto death. So when we feel humiliated by having to obey a mere mortal who may have a million sins, we can identify with Jesus in this and realize that he is giving us the pearl of great price.

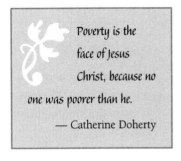

> *Poverty is the face of Jesus Christ, because no one was poorer than he.*
>
> — Catherine Doherty

When we become nothing, then we have everything.

He took our sins upon himself, so that we could be free from the bondage of sin.

Only the light of truth properly heals us. Sentimental love will not help any of us. We have to go through the veil into gospel love. Anything you find that helps you with this is blessed and honored.

As the struggle between good and evil mounts, the days will become clearer. Being victorious in our struggle does not matter—loving and trusting in our Lord matters. If in a moment of weakness you can get on your knees and pray, you will discover a small voice whispering inside of you, reminding you that you are totally and completely held in the palm of God the Father.

Let us choose childlikeness, so we can move quickly into this heart of love that desires only our good.

Everyone is aware of how crucial self-knowledge is. Self-knowledge leads to the realization that each of us is a sinner. This realization leads us to say, "Without God, *I can do nothing.*"

Wherever you are on this inner journey, *be at peace.* Each of us has been chosen through our baptism, and each of us must rest in the security that every little thing that happens today is for our good. This is why we cannot blame our brothers and sisters, but must mend the divisions in our own hearts. Then Our Lady of the Trinity can heal us, restore us, and sanctify us.

We must be patient with ourselves and one another. We must be tender, gentle, and understanding of our needs, as well as of the needs of our brothers and sisters.

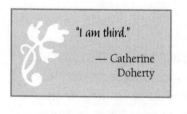

"I am third."

— Catherine
Doherty

The mounting difficulty of the *me*-centered universe is hitting every Christian all over the world, and the Holy Spirit is working overtime to clarify why God is first, my neighbor second, and I am third. The struggle is titanic, because of the massive breakdown in the Christian faith all over the world.

We are not dealing only with our personal patterns of sinful reaction or brokenness. We are dealing with generations of handed-down transmissions that are non-Christian or watered-down Christianity. This simply confirms Catherine's frequent lament, "I am up against a civilization."

A staff worker told a story about a man on a plane with claustrophobia. Telling someone that you're in distress is part of learning to deal with claustrophobia. It quickens healing and alleviates anxiety.

This man was in a state of panic, so he turned to the woman next to him and said, "Will you listen to me?"

"Of course," she replied.

He told her about his panic attack. As he did so, he looked into her eyes and saw in them a fear as deep and as terrible as his own. On instinct, he began to console her. He spoke softly, gently, and tenderly to her. He was soon relieved of his own fear.

Through giving the man was healed.

We are contemplatives in the marketplace. We must pray. All the action in the world will not bear the fruit that comes from a living awareness of and resting in the Trinity who dwells within us. We cannot shortcut the work that's underway to interiorize us.

Through purification after purification, and fidelity to God's will and the cross, Catherine was on fire with the presence of God and ready to begin this foundation by the time she came to Combermere. We, her sons and daughters, must know and believe that this is God's will for each of us. The magnitude of this fire will differ from person to person, but we must give our all. We must give everything for Jesus Christ who gave everything so that we could be free.

The saying Catherine used often, "Absence of the need to have becomes a need not to have,"[3] is a good benchmark for each of us. These words call for dispossession and detachment. The only thing we must not be detached from is God's Word and his living presence that comes through Baptism. There is no ultimate path to poverty. Take it for granted that you'll struggle. True poverty leads to the riches that only God can give.

I ask God every day for the grace to see only with his eyes, hear only with his ears, and love only with his heart. I hope we can all trust as never before, because so much is at stake in every little thing that we do, day in and day out. Forgiveness has to be multiplied until we are forgiving constantly all day long.

This meditation from St. Cyprian, a bishop in North Africa during the third century, is a word for us as we walk with joy through this time expectation of the Resurrection:

"Love those you previously hated. Show favor to those you previously envied. Imitate good people or at least rejoice with them in their virtue. Instead of cutting them off, make yourself their partner in the bond of fellowship. For your sins

---

3. Paul Evdokimov, *The Struggle With God* (Glen Rock NJ: Paulist Press, 1966), 123.

are forgiven only when you have forgiven others, and then you will be received by God in peace."

To prepare our hearts, let us forgive one another. Let us make a habit of always forgiving the simplest hurt, injury, rejection, or unkind word as it occurs during the day. Forgive until you can say with Jesus Christ, "Yes, I have forgiven seventy times seven."[4] When the day comes that we're able to say from the bottom of our hearts, "Father forgive every one, for they know not what they do," then we will be fitting instruments of love, joy, and peace for those who tumble into our houses. Let us get ready now!

Why, when we have such simple descriptive words from our Lord, are we so slow to be sanctified, divinized?

Many letters and countless one-to-one encounters remind me that the inner journey of repentance and conversion is not an end in itself. It's a gateway into what is absolutely vital for the unfolding of the Springtime of the Church.

The Holy Spirit reminded me that the Springtime will come when we no longer concentrate on our wounds, sinfulness, or pain. Only after we can drop these deeply embedded garments from childhood at the foot of the cross, do we begin to experience an exuberance of new life and joy. Only then do we begin to see our vocation with new eyes. Little flames will begin to appear, barely visible sometimes, but certainly there and growing. As we walk hand in hand and trust in God's mercy and work in us, the hidden flame of love will grow and grow until all of us as a body become a great bonfire.

4. Matthew 18:21–22

Chapter VII

Love's Unity

"For the Almighty has done great things
for me. Holy is his name."

— Luke 1:49

Let us join hands and pray this prayer from Catherine's heart:

"Lord, behold,

We are all kneeling here together,

Asking you to give us an increase of faith.

Let our hearts be open to you.

Let our heads be put into our hearts.

Let faith, hope, love, trust, and confidence reign among us.

Let us be done with human respect.

Let us be done with being afraid of ridicule.

Let us be done with thinking we have to hide anything
    from one another.

Lord behold,

We are in need of healing."[1]

Whatever purification is needed for each of us, individually and as a family, is underway. Fear nothing. The power of God's mercy will rush through your entire body, mind, heart, and soul with increasing vehemence in the days ahead. Expect miracles and new life, an increase of love and the fruit of the joy of the cross.

Now we must hold one another in prayer—and in our arms, if need be, so that the radiance of God's love will shine through us in ways that we can hardly hope for or imagine. We need to take deeply and seriously our reality as Christians.

Jesus Christ encompasses all of us. He encompasses East and West, North and South. He is here for every person of every nationality and color, who is walking the face of the

---

1. Doherty, "Touching God." In *Poustinia*, 130.

earth. We will be strained and purified in accepting others' cultural backgrounds, in the days to come. No matter where we go, we will be, first and foremost, Christians believing in Jesus Christ and knowing that our Savior is not an ideology. He is none other than God's gift of his beloved Son.

For each of us, we know that the battle is in our own hearts. The wisdom given to us through Catherine is needed more now than ever. When my heart is purified, when I'm flooded with faith, then I can be sure that perfect love will cast out all fear. In the meantime, look at fear not as an enemy but as the gateway into perfect and eternal union with our Lord Jesus Christ, the Father, and the Holy Spirit.

Go to Our Lady like a child and let her lead you today.

Unity in truth and love keeps coming into my mind and heart. Unity of East and West. Unity of diverse cultures—all plunged into a family of love that is born from the incarnation of the gospel.

Blessed John XXIII unleashed the advent of new life through calling into session the Second Vatican Council. What really transpired during those years is seen only dimly on the horizon. He followed his call to find the point of unity with fellow Christians. John Paul II echoes and reechoes that message in his own way. He doesn't hesitate to embrace the world and loves everyone while holding firm to truth.

Our heritage from Catherine is to transcend differences and see everyone and everything through the eyes of Jesus Christ. We have nothing to fear from any human being. The only enemy is the devil.

Globally, this is a time of tension between Evangelical groups and the Catholic Church. Let us pray that these mighty forces of the Christian body be united. Let us pray with Christ. Let us pray that Orthodox and Catholic believers forgive one another and love one another. The terrible break in the Body of Christ from the Reformation can begin to be healed. "Gather up the fragments lest they be lost." Are we not infused enough with love and truth to take one another by the hand and lift our voices with praise, gratitude, and honor to Almighty God?

> There is only one way to love God, and that is by loving your neighbor—the person next to you at any given moment. Turning your heart to Christ simply means turning to the one next to you at this moment in your life. Never forget that you shall be judged by love alone.
>
> — Catherine Doherty

We have been called into this incarnational love in a mighty, unprecedented way. Alone we get tossed by the wind and lose our moorings. But as a family, cannot an unceasing song of praise rise from our hearts as we do the dishes, prepare the gardens, clean the clothes, stack the wood, welcome the person who knocks at the door, answer the phone, write letters, listen to one another and to all who come to us? Can we not, from Russia through Asia, through North and South America, through the Islands, through Europe, and through Africa, one by one and all together, sing the praises of God as never before, so that the incredible reality of the Holy Trinity in each one of us will be lifted up and will strengthen our life?

Tensions and conflicts within the Church have been growing in increasing dimensions since Vatican II. These questions frequently come to my mind and heart:

Can we dare to hope that everyone is listening to the other?

Are we growing in the awareness that the other is the face of Jesus Christ?

Are we shedding the selfish "I" for the "thou"?

Are we daring to trust—to go out of our selfishness and to love and serve the other?

Are we daring to die to self, to give up all our controls and defenses so as to be free for the Kingdom of God to grow within?

Are we ready to enter the great white martyrdom so that we may experience the resurrection in our bodies?

Are we repenting daily so as to have a true conversion?

Ideas and opinions must flow from the mind of Christ. Communal life must bloom from the heart of Christ. Our union comes only in love.

The Holy Spirit moves uniquely in everyone. Because of that, we must never compare or judge one another's outward or inner life. We're often tempted to think that our brother and sister are failing to live out their vocations. We can protect the Apostolate by praying for anyone who seems to need a surge of zeal for this life. To allay this common temptation, St. John suggests,

"If anybody sees his brother commit a sin that is not a deadly sin, he has only to pray and God will give life to the sinner."[1]

1. 1 John:16–17

In essence, when we enter more fully into poverty, chastity, and obedience, we'll find our unity in diversity. Patience is crucial. Each person needs to be free to stand firmly rooted in the unique grace received for himself and to awaken his hunger and desire to live each particular aspect of Madonna House life. Frequent checking with one's director or spiritual director, or whoever can help, keeps us steadfast in our understanding and absorption of this life. We must all guard against murmuring, gossip, and comparisons. Little do we know what pain and struggle may be going on in our brother or sister's heart.

At the same time, we must cry out for the fire of desire to give ourselves totally in living each day.

Lord, are you preparing to return to Russia the incredible gift that we received from that land through Catherine?[2] Is there a deeper mystery of reunion and union taking place incarnationally than we can yet see? I believe that there are many staff workers already prepared to bring forth a new reality; they have plunged into their hearts and are standing still in the midst of incredible forces. Perhaps we are being formed into a communion of love, into a body that has not been seen in the Church for many centuries.

We know all too well the fragmentation, the rending of the body of Christ that has taken place through divisions. At this time in history, the Christian fragments seem endless.

---

2. Madonna House opened a field house in Magadan, Russia in 1994 based on the spirit Catherine received as a child in Russia.

Are we being asked to gather up the fragments of his body, just as we are gathering up the fragments of our own brokenness and placing these pieces at the foot of the cross? Are we being invited by Our Lady of the Trinity to walk hand in hand, 50 years ahead of the times, for the restoration of the Church? It may take 50 years, maybe even longer, for the fire of *sobornost* to radiate and enkindle the whole of Christendom, but some little group has to start it and it looks like we're it.

*W*e are in the era of *sobornost*. The veil has been lifted from our eyes. Stop and listen. Stop and listen, and find your center in the person of Jesus Christ, the Father, and the Spirit who dwell within.

*S*obornost is a mysterious unity that is vital for the Church today and in the future. It is the unity that Jesus Christ asked us to live when he prayed to the Father, "That they might all be one, as you are in me and I am in you."[3] To be in union with Jesus is the primary vocation of every Christian. Only in this union will every culture, tongue, and political body find unity. Externals cannot unify us across the globe, only the presence of Jesus can.

This real presence of Jesus through the Eucharist in us as Catholics is an incomparable reality that our fellow Christian friends of other post-Reformation denominations do not yet share. Even so, the Eucharist itself is the unifying factor that will gather up the fragments to unite every believer throughout the world. Jesus said, "I have come to bring all people to myself."[4] All those who know Jesus hunger for a deeper

3. John 17:22
4. John 12:32

experience of him, just as we do. We have not yet penetrated the depths of what God is calling us to.

In this age, when unity and peace are crucial to save the globe from destruction, the only answer is to give our whole life to the King. We need to trust our Lord and Master, Jesus Christ, as little children, and let him do what he wills to do with us. He holds our hands in his Mother's, so that we will be fearless in the days ahead. The exact day for the dawning of this new era of the purified Church is hidden in the mind and heart of God. We believe, we believe, we believe!

By gathering together and listening to one another, we find ways of perceiving and carrying one another, freed from obstacles that could hinder our walk together toward true *sobornost.*

During the years when Catherine was alive we were given the mantle of grace that comes through the living presence of a foundress. Before her death she tried to prepare us for this three-in-one fusion of laymen, laywomen, and

> *Love gives rise to the desire for unity, even in those who have never been aware of the need for it. . . . If we love one another, we strive to deepen our communion and make it perfect. Love is given to God as the perfect source of communion—the unity of Father, Son, and Holy Spirit—that we may draw from that source the strength to build communion between individuals and comm-unities, or to re-establish it between Christians still divided.*
>
> — John Paul II,
> *Ut Unum Sint*

priests.[5] We have done an enormous amount of work in communication and loving one another, and in the practical, arduous effort of bending, listening, and moving into one another. When Catherine died the direction of the family moved from the era of the foundress into the era of *soborno-st*. This is not a manmade concept; it is a gift and a reality that comes from the Holy Spirit. God has honored our daily efforts at loving him and one another.

It is the Lord who builds this house of love. We go to Catherine for materials that make up the height, depth, width, and strength of this house, but it is designed by God. It is for his creation, love, and mercy, and always for others. Each of us must walk into our own inward journeys with confidence.

We know that God is wrestling with each of us, to bring a much deeper sense of responsibility for our vocation. He is wresting from us a surrender, so that the future will be cemented more deeply than ever in the heart of our foundress and in the Little Mandate.

Sobornost is the charism of this era, on an incarnational level. We have and will continue to do inner work but communally we must shift our gaze more and more to God alone. See every little thing in daily life as God asking us to turn to him in trust. This is a communal affair and is the means by which we will be set on fire. It must begin in our hearts, one by one, in trust, surrender, and in the darkness of faith.

5. Madonna House, in embracing *sobornost,* is called to be three separate branches living in a total unity of mind, heart, and soul—one family.

We can liken *sobornost* to a flow of love in the light of the Mystical Body of Christ. That means that we are all in this together. We reflect one body, one mind, one heart, one spirit. There is no "star," so to speak, but only the incarnation of love that must grow until we are totally the reflection of Jesus Christ.

We are *mandated* by God to be a *sobornost*, a unity of mind and heart, between laymen, laywomen, and priests. As we know, humanly speaking, this is impossible. It is really original sin that we are being asked to transform. Let us pray for humility and courage. Let us pray that we be released from anything that imprisons us. We each still are in a prison of one kind or another, be it of bamboo bars or solid steel. God wants us liberated.

Sobornost is absolutely impossible for human beings to achieve. Yet it can easily be achieved by gathering together and focusing on one purpose—finding and doing God's will, not our own; not passing on our own ideas, good as they may be. We may express our opinions but then we ask ourselves, "Now what is God's will in this matter?" When we all want to do God's will, *sobornost* will take place in a beautiful, simple, childlike, easy way.

How often we forget that, without Jesus, we cannot love anyone or anything as they are meant to be loved. But he reminds us that the Eucharist is not simply for ourselves. It is the foundation on which we are able to love one another. We need to remind ourselves and one another that it is the Eucharist, along with the unifying presence of the Holy Spirit among us, that allows us to become one body, one mind, one heart. Daily each one of us needs to remind ourselves of what the sacramental life does in us, with us, and through us.

What seems like an impossible challenge—*sobornost*—is made possible through the Eucharist. The Eucharist coupled with Confession, wherein we forgive ourselves and our neighbor, and receive the forgiveness of God, permits the enlargement of our heart in ways that we can hardly imagine.

The hunger for God is growing in all of our hearts. The sword of pain is piercing more deeply into our hearts, so that we can complete the work God has given us. Never in the history of the Church has there been such a call given for *sobornost*.

In this age, when division, hatred, and the fallout of original sin have splintered the body of Christ into many fragments, we, the little ones of God, have been chosen to help restore this unity of love and peace. Our greatest contribution is our littleness, humility, and childlikeness. The rest God is more than happy to do for us and in us.

Our lives hang by a thread. The only crucial tasks right now are to trust, surrender, and stay infinitely faithful to whatever daily responsibility God gives us. God is in control of everything. If we can love one another as we have been told to love by Jesus, we will come out of multi-layered difficulties with greater faith, and will be closer to what we all desire—a true *sobornost*.

We bandy about the word "*sobornost*" without understanding its implications. It is God's mandate to us. It is God's gift
to us. We cannot make it happen. It must be done unto us
according to his word. Our Lady shows us the way. I beg you
to make a good confession, so that no divisiveness, no thread
of selfishness, no sinfulness can mar whatever God wants to
do for us.

True *sobornost* will come through the Holy Spirit. Perhaps
the Spirit is telling us to come to Our Lady more quickly
these days, because she, with her spouse, will open new
paths as we continue our walk together into the depths of
inner unity of mind and heart.

The crux of the matter is that God loves us and that it
requires understanding, trust, and courage to enter into
sobornost.

In order for our prayers to be powerful, we must be united
in the simplicity of the Little Mandate and in our love for one
another. If unity and pulling together is incarnated—devoid
of division and without separation between male and
female—then our Lord, the Father, the Spirit, and Our Lady
will honor and abundantly bless us. Unity has never been
more crucial. We flesh out the gospel in a most extraordinary
way by being rooted in the nitty-gritty of everyday life. That's
something that all of Christendom needs.

The positive and negative signs of communal life surfaced again this week.

Positive signs included unity, childlikeness, and no strong personalities.

The negative signs were confusion, poor communication, and potential for divisiveness.

To read these signs we must realize that the enemy is unhappy with how we daily and valiantly work at living the gospel without compromise.

The enemy's distractions will not stop. They'll probably escalate. So rejoice if you have trials, temptations, and inner struggles. Be watchful, be prayerful, and run quickly to the Mother of God for protection. Pull together whenever a crisis occurs, little or big. Take one another by the hand and stand firm. You'll be given the light you need, just for today.

When God is at work, you can be sure the enemy is nearby and eager to destroy what God is building. Be on your guard. Cover yourself daily with prayers of protection. Be quick to forgive one another and seal off any potential divisions that may lurk in daily life. Do not let the sun go down without forgiving everyone who has hurt you.

It is love who is building this house. We are the fragile vessels that heaven has chosen to bring forth the face of love to all who come to our blue doors.

This morning I went to the dictionary and looked up "perseverance." To persevere means "to persist in any enterprise *in spite of counter influences or opposition.*" This closely fits three words currently in the air:

Fear—a painful emotion marked by alarm; dread; disquiet.

Tension—the act of stretching; state or degree of being strained to stiffness.

Discouragement—to be lessened in the courage of; to be disheartened; state of being deterred.

We know God constantly loves us, no matter what we think, feel, or do. Our *raison d'etre* is to be loved by him. Like a child we must look every day at fear, tension, and discouragement, if they are plaguing us, and ask, "What is God giving me in the midst of this? What door inside of me is he trying to enter?" The light of faith shines upon the words, "fear," "tension," and "discouragement" and gives us answers. Perseverance comes through finding some means of counteracting our obstacles.

You can transform your fear by surrender. Our purification in daily life comes by a simple act of surrender to the invisible God who constantly loves us. Fear can be transformed.

Tension is transformed by stretching—by being stretched into new love, new life, a new breakthrough. Most tension is provoked through associating with one another. There may be tension between two people. There's often palpable tension within our houses. There's tension caused by things going on in the world. We can turn tension into growth by being stretched into greater love.

Is not discouragement a lack of courage? Not that we can conjure up courage on our own. That's why we have the gift of fortitude. It has to come from God. Through the power of the Holy Spirit, God comes to our aid at times of discouragement. Stand still and quickly make a silent plea for help from the Holy Spirit. When you are discouraged, pray, "Give me fortitude, please. I need your courage for I am weak and needy at this moment."

Why are we afraid? Because we are not united with God, and therefore we cannot be united with our brothers and sisters. So what do we do in pain? Every day when you wake up in the morning and go to bed at night, restore your primary unity of love with Our Lady of the Trinity. Then our relationships will come into order.

It behooves us to consecrate ourselves each day and to pray the simple prayer of Our Lady of Combermere. Every house is a room in her heart. Nothing divides us. Her love and her Son's love unite us.

> The Mother of God will comfort you. Her voice is like oil on a wounded heart. No matter how dark the night, there will be light because Mary will be there.
>
> — Catherine Doherty

The purifying fire of love comes to us through pain, so that his joy and his love may be made manifest in all of us.

Know that everything that is happening to you today is allowed and permitted for your good, so that you can be cleansed, purified, and transformed by the all-merciful love of God, himself. Remember we are all in this together. When you suffer I suffer. When you are in peace, I am in peace.

When you love I receive that love. When you are in pain, that pain comes into my heart. We give and receive. Our deepest point of unity is tangibly clear, and that is the hearts of Jesus and Mary.

We are part of the mystical body of Christ and we carry in silence and hiddenness the sufferings and the joys of all baptized Catholics.

There is no separation in the body of Christ. When one is in sorrow, all are in sorrow. When one is in joy, all of us are in a state of rejoicing.

Atonement leads to the essence of love. Seeds of love's reality begin to sprout as soon as we see that when my brother suffers, I suffer, when my brother is in joy, I am in joy.

In the West, we constantly run up against our cultural inheritance of individualism. Night and day we need to labor against the *I* and become the *we*. It is taking, and will take, patience and time to see the body of Christ with eyes of faith, rather than as me, Mary, John, Sue, David. But we're on the road.

On the level of getting through daily life, interrelating, and practical things, we've become experts. Now, together and one by one, we're developing a deeper family life by entering into the mystical body of Christ through the power of the Father, Son, and Holy Spirit. This requires deeper purification and trust in God and one another. Let nothing knock us off this path. The magnitude of the vision extending before us is breathtaking.

An understanding of the interconnectedness of all living things is growing, both from realizing the Christian perspective and from the knowledge accumulating because of the grace of our Lord's presence in the world. The power of the death and resurrection of our Lord and Savior Jesus Christ cannot be stopped, ever. Whether people believe or not, the movement of God that's reclaiming his people and his creation will continue until every word our Lord spoke is fulfilled.

When one surrenders totally, it affects the whole family. When a body of people surrenders to God, it not only affects the whole family, it affects the whole world. This corporate body of believers is growing deeper in faith, hope, and love. Along with this growth and with our surrender, dedication, loyalty, and commitment, comes an escalation in the struggle between powers and principalities. Always remember that. When we are doing something beautiful for God, the enemy does everything possible to discourage and dissuade us, and puts clouds of any possible kind over our life.

God has honored our repentance. Love has grown here this past year. Now we are ready to enter into this great feeding on God himself that he offers to us every day at the Liturgy.

Pray for interior silence when you enter the doors of the Church. When you receive the Lord through the Eucharist, it is the most intimate union of love known to human beings on this earth. No sexual act, no friendship, no personal prayer, can even come close to the union of God with each one of us when we are at the Liturgy.

The heart of the life of Jesus Christ takes place at the Liturgy. We are given what provides the fullness of life here on earth and for all eternity. The Christian world one day will come back to the realization of what this sacrament means.

We must bless every atheist, Muslim, Jew, Hindu, Buddhist, Christian, even those who worship Satan. Bless everyone, because everyone came from the mind and heart of the Father, and his only begotten Son came to show us the way home.

Many other Christians are giving us insights into facets of our Catholic heritage that we've minimized, forgotten, or not exercised. Ultimately, in and through his presence at Mass, our Lord and Savior Jesus Christ will draw all men to himself.

Let us pray for one another and see with new eyes how each one of us is a vital part of this great mystical body of Christ, given to us through his Church.

Pray daily for more faith, hope, and love. Our God is lavishing each one of us with truth and love according to the unique creation each one of us is. Therefore we can never look at one another with envy or jealousy lest we mar the icon of our Lord's presence in our heart. Help one another. Accept one another. Pray for one another.

The inner work goes on day after day, week after week, month after month. It is going to be with us until the day we die, but the positive element in this is that as we exercise the power of God's presence living in us, and we increase our trust in him, somehow the joy of the struggle grows side by side with the painful elements. We are confident in the reality of our oneness and growing love for one another, and our growing confidence that God's mercy is taking hold.

It takes the fire of God. It takes the faith of the saints. It takes the all-consuming love of each one of us to bring to completion the great calling in life that has been given to us. We must move, for there is little time. We must keep our eyes on our destiny, which is sanctification, divinization, transformation. We must look at our God to know who we are as individuals. We must take the road of the gospel or we will perish.

Being emptied so as to be filled with God gives us that hunger and desire to lay our lives down for him and for one another. We are called to martyrdom so that all of us, and the whole world, can ultimately become one in Jesus Christ.

Chapter VIII

Personal Dignity

*"And his faithful love extends age after age
to those who fear him."*

— Luke 1:50

Teach us, your little ones,
always to reflect on
and recognize your presence in us.
Teach us to go quickly to you
in the Blessed Sacrament
and reconnect with you
when we're unmoored.
Teach us to so realize
your coming into our bodies at Communion
that nothing
can deter us from our faith
and our belief that you live in us
at that moment and for all eternity.

There can be no joy without pain. They're companions. Pain and joy, pain and love, pain and life always go hand in hand.

When we're in the midst of pain, we're prone to look at it and forget there's a reason for it. And it's not because we're bad. It's because God is bringing forth something that needs to be restored, renewed, and made whole again.

The secret of pain and joy living together is surrender. We all experience pain in this life. Until we learn the secret of surrender to pain, we live in anguish, constantly striving to get ourselves out of this terrible sense of having the wind knocked out of us or not being able to go on. When we surrender, trusting like a little child, the pain doesn't disappear, but God takes this pain that is now wedded to him and produces a blend of joy and pain in our hearts and in our souls. This is the secret of the saints.

During a time of exposure of the root causes of our own woundedness and sinfulness, we cannot help but uncover pain, the source of which comes from original sin. Gradually we must learn how to live with that pain so that God himself can bring forth its blending with his cross, which produces in each of us a mysterious joy that no one can ever take from us.

We need to drop the negative connotation of pain that causes us, when we're in pain, to feel that, "I must be bad, I must be doing something wrong, there is something ugly and unlovable in me." That's wrong thinking!

Pain is an inevitable mark of the Christian life, because it is the place where God himself is able to transform the old creature into a new creation. Pain is the refining fire of the Holy Spirit. Therefore, when we feel this pain, we should trust that the suffering is a crucible and that what will come forth will be more beautiful, more pure, more worthy of God.

But this is not the only consolation that pain bestows upon our soul. Jesus Christ is holy. He sanctified pain by his contact with it. He desired to make use of pain to redeem the human race. As often as we suffer, we complete the Passion of Christ.

There is absolutely no possibility of us having union with God, except through the joy of the cross. We all know this theoretically. But when we are in the incarnational process of this, we sometimes come close to despair and wonder: will it ever end? Believe me, it will end. And that's where we have to help one another, stand by one another, pray for one another, and seek a wise guide when we are in the midst of it. No one can go through this alone, unless they have extraordinary graces.

It's clear that the press does not give much news from a Christian perspective; therefore all of us have to be vigilant and in touch with other sources that reflect what the Church says about vital questions, about technology that's moving more rapidly than anyone cares to say. In the last hundred years, the acceleration of life has left everyone breathless.

Our life, which calls us to go into the depths of our hearts and launch out into deep faith, is becoming more important than ever. With conflicts, violence, and immorality flowering, it is all the more pressing for us to cull the weeds from our own hearts and cleanse the places where we aren't loving, forgiving, and embracing our brother and sister. It's never been more important in the history of the world for us to receive through the Eucharist, through the Word, through prayer, the magnificent mercy of the Father, Son, and Holy Spirit.

> Each of us exists, even as Mary did, to give birth to Christ in us.
>
> — Catherine Doherty

Yesterday at the Divine Liturgy, the Archbishop said that only the Mother of God stands as our prophet, leading us all into the fullness of Divine Life. She was the chosen one to receive from the Father the incredible invitation to allow Jesus into her humanity, thus bringing the Divine Life into this world. The incarnation all began with her. We are under her protection and under her mantle. The glory of the Risen Lord cannot come into its full stature without her. We go to her like children and allow her to give us what we need each day.

Through the years, we've groped our way through incidents and situations where we had to trust the Holy Spirit. At this particular time in the history of the world, it's obvious that the brokenness of our masculinity and femininity is deep and in need of great attention. It's amazing how there is a body of knowledge and expertise being given to us from counselors of all kinds who have unlocked many difficulties for us. The pain involved in it all is great. There is also shame, humiliation, and fear that have to be faced. To be truly chaste, as a little family of God, is counter cultural in the 21st century.

Years ago, two books touched me deeply, *Human Destiny* by Lecomte du Nouy and *Man and Society in Calamity* by Sorokin.

Lecomte du Nouy won a Nobel Prize in physics. His little volume was written in the 1920s. One sentence changed my life: "The greatest genius or the highest level of genius in the world is the saint." We think of Mozart, Beethoven, Picasso, Einstein. We think of all kinds of geniuses and outstanding world figures that have changed the history of mankind. But this sentence shocked me into the reality that everyone who is a baptized Christian can become the very highest degree of genius in all of creation—a saint. And that is exactly what our vocation is all about. So, wherever you are, you can stop and say, "My life today is of infinitely more importance than any occupation I could have chosen in the secular world."

Sorokin is the father of sociology. In his work, he describes the different stages of society. According to him, we go from the sensate into a high degree of spiritual life; he gives three different levels. In essence he says that in uneventful times, when history is more stable, we live in shades of gray. As the sensate culture takes over, there is a breaking off whereby some persons strive to regain or rediscover the spiritual meaning of life itself.

This is probably why so many are searching today in the highways and byways of the world for meaning. Certainly, there is an insatiable hunger for meaning in life and to be in contact with spiritual realities. Many have been duped into searching for reality in false spiritualities. The New Age movement is perhaps the foremost model of a false spiritual life with us today. All the more reason why we Christians need to persevere in total confidence and trust in our Baptism.

*W*hat you do is important but who you are in the eyes of God is far more important. Let us not mistake this—our priority is the person. At the same time, we have to return to the simplicity of God's order by trusting in the "grace of state" of those in authority over us, and trusting in the duty of the moment.

*E*very hair on your head has been counted."[1] This is how close the Father, the Son, and the Spirit are to each of us. God draws us quickly and with certainty into the center of his heart and his Mother's. For each person that movement is unique, sacred, and different from anyone else's experience. Have confidence in that reality and put all your trust in God.

1. Luke 12:7

We are not imitators of Catherine's life. We walk in her footsteps through our unique temperament, experiences, and receptivity to the Trinity's presence in us, for the fleshing out of the vision God wants for Madonna House. But we have to be marinated or seasoned in this receptivity to God, after we have gone through a rather intense and ongoing formation within the life of the family itself.

It's an exciting time. It's a joy to know that we're slowly but surely entering into one of the most exciting journeys of faith, not only for ourselves, but for all generations to come. How God plays on each person's heart is unique. There will never be two members of this family who will have the same story to tell, but the pattern will bear threads of great similarity, because when the Holy Spirit, the Father, and the Son are doing the work within us, you can be sure the fleshing out of the divine will bring us into a unity that we can hardly imagine. We must become more Christ-centered, for our rest will come through that.

The winds of disturbance seem to be subsiding a little, but they

> Perhaps one of the most glaring weaknesses of present-day civilization lies in an inadequate view of the human being. Undoubtedly our age is the age that has written and spoken the most about the human being. ... But paradoxically it is also the age of people's deepest anxieties about their identity and destiny; it is the age when human beings have been debased to previously unsuspected levels, when human values have been trodden underfoot as never before.
>
> — John Paul II,
> *Puebla Conference address*

will blow again. Have courage. Support and encourage one another. Make sure you don't blame or judge. Take your burdens to Jesus Christ.

The universal call to repentance and conversion is deepening everywhere. The push to take responsibility for our own wounding and sinfulness is growing day by day, as we experience more hidden graces that lead to confidence in an individual interior liberation, as well as communal liberation. We are to be a fire, a blazing fire, of God's love wherever we are. This is work that has to be done through the Holy Spirit, but it is rooted in the great gift we receive through the Eucharist.

We all have been relieved and strengthened, because we have been given light and insight about many of our struggles in living so closely together, through disciplines that have come from the Christian body. We all know that ultimately God is the one who heals us. We've acquired many blocks and blindnesses from a very broken civilization, but the Holy Spirit is giving light to the Christian body. We're no longer simply dealing with the psychological phenomena. Our understanding has deepened into a wedding of the spiritual and the material, so that the light of grace is able to help us change destructive patterns within our individual lives. We are grateful for this grace.

Take a moment to look at one another. God has created you with two eyes, a nose, and a mouth. Yet, how unique is each face—never to be repeated again.

This is a manifestation of God's great love for us and of his endless creative power forming us. If we can keep our eyes on this creative power of the Holy Spirit working in and through us, we will delight in, wonder at, admire, and be in awe of all of our brothers and sisters.

As long as our reality centers around the me-myself-and-I, we stay bound. Our reflection of true self only comes by looking at the face of Jesus Christ. If you want to know who you are, look at the face of Jesus Christ and let your mind be filled with his truth so that your heart can sing.

Joy, peace, and love have come into the hidden recesses of our heart, where the Holy Spirit is working twenty-four hours a day to cleanse us and free us from anything that is not of the gospel.

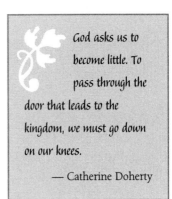

God asks us to become little. To pass through the door that leads to the kingdom, we must go down on our knees.

— Catherine Doherty

The more we see with the eyes of the gospel and with the eyes of the Church, the more our life together will be shot through with truth and love.

We are a little, unimportant, and hidden family. To God, we are of infinite importance. He has mandated us to carry the gospel without compromise. The hunger of human hearts that has been recently exposed asks us to step out in joy and faith. If you are doing ordinary jobs all day today, your hands and your heart can touch China, India, America, and every person in need, through wedding your yes in love with that of our Lord and his Mother. It's that simple.

Each of us has a unique place in the family of man—a place no one else can take. Each of us in the nitty-grittiness of our daily lives plays a vital part in fleshing out the revolution of love that is in process. We do not know what's in God's mind and heart. But we can be sure that every day we will be challenged to be more flexible, and ready to allow the painful penetration and purifying light of the Holy Spirit to enter us.

Let us bow low and pray for deep humility, hiddenness, and inner silence.

There is no way to fulfill this desire we all carry, except to keep before us the face of our Beloved and to shield our eyes from the weakness and sinfulness of one another.

The only heart to be transformed is our own. Hope will fortify and give us new life in the days ahead because our charism is *love*.

Let us rest in the peace of Christ and love one another. Repent, every day, of judgment and negativity against yourself, against your neighbor, and against God. The price has been paid through the glory of Good Friday; its link to Easter is eternal. The two blend into the greatest song of love the world has ever heard. We are, through Baptism, eternally wedded to this mystery.

Chapter IX

God's Children

*"He has used the power of his arm,
he has routed the arrogant of heart."*

— Luke 1:51

When you're tempted to anger or to judge anyone, put this little prayer into your heart instead:

> Lord, I give you
> this person. . .
> and this person. . .
> and ask you to help them.
> Please, give me
> only unconditional love
> at this moment.

Mother Teresa is a woman of rare courage, love, humility, and truth, who has brought the supernatural answer to this world gripped in the culture of death. How do you contend with her love for the dying, the lepers, the homeless, and the crippled—for the rejects of the earth? She herself was vilified by some people. But what is that in the face of the gospel message of love that fell upon believers and unbelievers of every race, nation, and tribe. She lifted the poor of humanity and offered them kindness, security, and love as if they were the very presence of Jesus Christ in her arms.

Whatever parts of our hearts still carry fear, darkness, or uncertainty are being challenged by faith. We cannot be emptied and enter into the heart of God, who is all love, unless we trust and surrender in faith, in darkness, and often in pain. If you are experiencing any of these three qualities know that you are being called higher. Shed whatever clings to the places that God desires to fill with himself.

If, as a family, we surrender unconditionally as the Mother of God did, we will receive like a blaze of fire the love, mercy, peace, and joy only God can give.

I beg you to open up the door of your heart and be filled with expectancy to receive more and more graces. Ask for what you need, and thank God for every joy and every pain that comes your way. Praise him with exultant song from the depths of your heart.

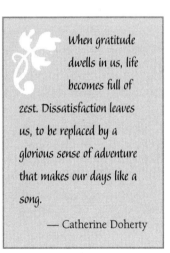

When gratitude dwells in us, life becomes full of zest. Dissatisfaction leaves us, to be replaced by a glorious sense of adventure that makes our days like a song.

— Catherine Doherty

It's only when we are pushed into corners, where there are no answers, that we can finally yield like a child to the mercy of God.

Let us constantly remind our-selves that God permits every-thing that happens to us, for our good. Simply shift your focus and become aware that everything that's happening to you and within you is the purifying love of the Holy Spirit. This will transform pain into joy, death into life, and dis-couragement into courage.

The ability to open things up, as a family, was a major step in our growing in love. It takes courage to speak the truth in love. It takes humility to receive the truth with surrender.

The moment has come when we can be bold and demand that God fill us with growing love for one another and ourselves. We surrender all we are and all we hope to be, like little children, into his Mother's hands. Our family life is growing because we all desire God.

Do we have inner work to do? You bet your life we do! But hope comes in knowing that we are all accepted as we are—wounds, warts, and whatever. The great work of this time in our life as a family is this communal purification and self-emptying. In God's timetable will come not only restoration but the greatest outpouring of the Holy Spirit that we have ever known.

The glory of God is upon you because of your faithfulness, your perseverance in faith in your own particular duty of the moment. Stand firm, and God will bless us all abundantly with his glory as the need arises.

The fact that we are living such an ordinary life and are constantly faced with repetitive daily tasks can be very wearying on a natural level, unless we have vision. It will be wearisome unless we can see deeply into the ramifications of all the things that we're doing day by day, and can constantly refocus our minds and hearts on what is really essential. So I ask you to simply chew on these words and let them help you turn your face to the cross and the resurrection of our Lord and Savior, Jesus Christ.

Each of us is on a personal journey, as well as a communal journey. Although God's action never ceases, we can remain in God's will and increase the depth of unity that he so desires only by staying focused on the essentials. Essentially, we're here to love God with our whole mind, our whole heart, and our whole soul, and to love one another.

The witness of love has never been more needed. Wherever we are, anyone who comes to us is certain to have been deeply affected by the culture of death prevalent throughout the world. This culture of death zaps the life out of the spirit. To counteract this, we must be more alert and vigorous in focusing on the essentials of our own spiritual lives. Otherwise, having one foot in the secular world and one foot in the spiritual world will tear us apart.

There is an ongoing temptation to have the best of both worlds. That's impossible. God slowly and persistently culls and peels away all of those areas in our mind, our psyche, our heart, every part of our being, that want to cling to the kingdom of the world instead of the kingdom of God. Don't be surprised when you are challenged by things you thought were settled. They won't be settled until you see God face to face.

If we don't grow in trust minute by minute and day by day, then we won't find what our hearts seek, which is God. God alone can satisfy the hunger of our hearts. No amount of counseling, no friend, no place, nothing will satisfy us but the presence of God dwelling in us. For this to happen, we must be emptied and we don't like that. It's painful and it demands an enormous amount of trust.

One of the first things Catherine said to me was, "Grace builds on nature." Nature has moved far from the reality of God's original creation. Our work is to become restored in our hearts, souls, and spirits. Healing is simply the process of removing the obstacles that keep us from seeing clearly who God is and who we are as creatures in relationship to him.

> A "fool for Christ's sake" can go anywhere, because people will laugh at him but will let him in.
>
> — Catherine Doherty

Rejoice in your poverty, weakness, emptiness, and humanity. Trust that without God you can do nothing. Confidently call down the mercy of God, who is thirsting to transform us into a new creation for his glory and for our own harmony as brothers and sisters. Let God love you.

Already the light of a new creativity is shining within us. We will slowly see the unfolding of the resplendence of the Church. We will be transformed as we walk hand in hand into the restoration of the Church—East and West.

It behooves all of us to ponder, pray, and exercise our capacity to bless one another in our hearts and minds, so that we can transmit love constantly to everyone in faith and in trust.

For it is only the Church, resurrected and glorious, that can bring true peace and love back to this earth.

Our freedom as children of God allows us to carry the stamp of life that far outweighs the forces that could oppress, dominate, and control us. We must have growing confidence that this creative energy will grow and grow as we transmit love to one another.

We, who are small, have been shown the face of the Infant. This Infant, who is our Savior, was hidden in Nazareth for 30 years, then walked the roads to proclaim the Good News, died on a cross, and rose again. What does he tell us? Everything can be destroyed except love. That love is in you and no one can take it from you. Have confidence, have courage, and become true adorers through the power of Jesus Christ.

Let us begin. Let us hunger and thirst to know the living God. Let us rejoice in every joy and in every sorrow. Let us be exultant, so that when Christmas dawns, we may rush like little children to proclaim to the four corners of the earth that

Christ is glorified. He has come! Nothing can destroy this enormous gift of himself to each of us.

The Mother of God wants her presence and her maternal tenderness to come into greater focus for all her children. It is she who will give us the security, protection, and love that everyone needs in super abundance to follow her son. I urge you to pray to her very simply, as a child would. Begin simple tasks with a movement of your heart, asking her to be by your side.

We can, like children, do little things well for the love of God. We can receive everyone as Christ. We can open up the chambers of our heart and rest with confidence in the great love of Our Lady. We can be bold in proclaiming the way, the truth and the life, through doing what we're asked to do, or through proclaiming it in words. Either way, God will be present in and through our fidelity.

We are called to live by love, not by the law. The more we're able to chip away at our fear, our controls, and especially our fear of making mistakes, the more we will become free to simply live like little children in this place that has been designed for restoration of the gospel way of life.

Catherine was relentless in connecting everything to the gospel. We must do the same.

How blessed we are to be chosen, to be invited, to be permitted to cry the gospel with our life. Let us all walk to the crib as little children, hand in hand, and kneel before this God-child, who allowed himself to fall into the hands of humanity. What a trust he has in us! Pray that we can trust him more and more, and can know that God is with us, God is in us, and that God is leading us into something that is eternal.

Faith is taking hold of the gospel and incarnating it in every corner of life.

Don't look too much at the darkness around us, don't get pulled down by the culture of death. Keep your eyes lifted up to the mountaintop. Keep your eyes filled with the vision of life that has been given to us—our life and true inheritance. As Archbishop Raya says so often, "You become what you contemplate."

Beauty, love, life, goodness, and truth will feed your heart and soul with what is eternal and everlasting. Pain will strengthen you. The joy of the cross will give you the courage to walk day by day into tomorrow, no matter what comes. Pray for faith. All you have to do is ask.

All things that happen to us are gifts from God. We must have the eyes to see what goodness, beauty, truth, love, and joy will be brought into them through the creative force of God himself, if we attach ourselves to him with the total confidence of a child.

At our gathering recently an enormous amount of restless, emotional energy was provoked, because we were just beginning to grasp how fragile the male-female relationship is. Since then we have done enormous work in this area, but we still have quite a bit to learn. Our hearts are open, less fearful, and eager to pursue this celibate relationship that is an important part of our family life. Others have told us they are astounded at what we're trying to do, since there's no exact model in the Church for us to follow. We are plowing and harrowing untried soil. We have to keep perspective. Don't be afraid to make mistakes. Relationships are often messy. This is normal.

Prayer is growing in Madonna House. Spiritual warfare is no less fierce than it has been at other times in our history, but we are growing in confidence and trust that we are the children of God and have nothing to fear. We are growing in confidence that we are pilgrims on this earth. We cannot hesitate as we spend our lives, for we know that many souls are at stake, and in need of our small but tender and loving deeds and actions.

I see a kaleidoscope of ingenuity and creativity, and how radically different the Holy Spirit works in each of us. The word that keeps coming to my mind and heart is, "Gather up the fragments lest they be lost."

We're confident in our unique way of reflecting the mystical body of Christ, simply through our very small family life. When we can see, hear, and appreciate one another at the level of watching God work in such different ways, our vision opens to the whole Church, and we accept and bow before every nationality, every expression of the uniqueness of our Lord, living in and through all of his children.

I would say that our gathering up of the fragments shows us magnificent pictures of something way beyond ourselves as individuals, and gives us courage to love and appreciate one another in a much deeper fashion.

Begin to see how everything we touch, say, and do is an extension of the God of love. Could we not this year make a resolution to stand like children every morning and receive the unending power of God's love into our hearts, so that it can move through us to everyone and everything that constitutes our duty of the moment for today? Remember, we have nothing except this moment. Let it be a moment rooted in love.

We are the spoiled children of the Holy Trinity, living in Our Lady's house. How blessed we are to be chosen by Jesus Christ to follow in his footsteps. How blessed we are to be chosen to follow in the footsteps of our foundress. How blessed we are to have such a lavish gift of

> Every Sunday, the Risen Christ asks us to meet him as it were once more in the Upper Room where, on the "evening of the first day of the week" (John 20:19) he appeared to his disciples in order to "breathe" on them his life-giving Spirit and launch them on the great adventure of proclaiming the Gospel.
>
> — John Paul II, *Novo Millennio Ineunte*

faith, hope, and love at our disposal, every minute of every day. How blessed we are to have been chosen to be baptized, to be confirmed, and to be temples of God himself.

What a gift it is to be a Catholic. What a gift it is to know that every day we can run like little children to ask our Father to forgive us for all of our waywardness. What a gift the Church gives us to receive again and again the very Body and Blood of our Lord and Savior, Jesus Christ.

If we don't know anything else, we know that without God we can do nothing, but with God, watch out! We are the glory of the risen Lord, and the risen Lord is beating firmly and splendidly in the heart of each one of us. We must be careful to never allow the weight of our humanity and the imperfection of our daily lives to stand in the way of the true reality of our calling.

I ask all of you to pray the Our Father with fervor every day. Meditate upon it and deepen your awareness of the words of the only prayer that Jesus gave us when he walked the earth. It may take a year or five years to really plummet the depths of that simple prayer that we often recite quickly, easily, and without letting it penetrate into our hearts.

How blessed we are! How blessed we are to have the Eucharist every day. How blessed we are to have one another. Remember Catherine's story—when she was a little girl, she said to her mother, "I want to touch God," and her mother replied, "Touch me."

Chapter X

Reaching Out

"He has pulled down princes from their thrones and raised high the lowly."

— Luke 1:52

Our Lord is waiting for us to say,

> "With you
> All things are possible.
> I believe,
> I trust,
> And I will love,
> Never counting the cost."

We are called to restore in a particular way the modern marketplaces in the world. Death to self through *kenosis* is crucial.

This is what Catherine has to say about being transformed and bearers of the gospel as lay people:

"We are a new breed of contemplatives. Our monasteries are the busy streets of new pagan cities, the noisy thoroughfares of immense metropolises that sing the hymns of the world, the flesh, and the devil. Our convents are rural roads, deserted because they are no longer traveled by men who know and love God.

"We are a new breed of contemplatives, whose prayer is accompanied by clanging sirens, honking horns, blaring radios and tramping feet. We are a new breed of contemplatives, and our bells are the poor, knocking ceaselessly at our blue doors. We are a new breed of contemplatives, and we must learn to rest on the heart of God, listening to the perfect harmony of his heartbeats while we go about his business in the midst of the most discordant music the world has ever known."

As society crumbles around you, you must grow in confidence and courage, knowing that nothing can separate you from the love of Jesus Christ. Our strength lies in our unity, and that unity comes only through the life of Jesus Christ leading, guiding, and moving through us. At least once a day Catherine would say to me, "It is not what you do that matters, but what God does in you and through you." I pass that wisdom on to you. Don't worry about your emotions, or your status, or your weakness. It is totally unimportant. What does matter is *love*. From that will come peace into all of our hearts and into the world. There *is* no other way.

Every time we step out and ask our friends to help, they too become lay apostles. Let us pass this on more and more as time goes by. We must reach out to everyone who comes to our houses and inspire them to cry the gospel with their lives. By asking them to help us, the fire starts.

The word that has pounded in my heart all week is: *Stop, look, listen! Be alert, be watchful, listen!*

This whole rhythm of inner and outer movement is ceaseless, as long as we're walking the face of this earth. We have to say, "What is God saying through the people he sends to us? Why is he sending them?" They come because they are seeking God. They are seeking a place where they can be restored. They are coming for reasons that are known only to Jesus and his Mother. We have to be very prayerful and reverent toward the people who come through our blue doors.

We do not exist for our own comfort or for our own self-development, but for our beings to be restored through the winnowing fan of the Father, Son, and Holy Spirit. And so we, today, are building a house of love through joy and through pain. These are the endless cycles of our life, whether we're here or any other place in the world. It is Our Lady and her Son who are really reigning as King and Queen over each and every one of us, for the restoration of the world to the gospel.

The earth is troubled. Who will restore it, if we do not begin today? Do not waste time looking at your neighbor. Focus your mind and heart on God, and then your eyes will be cleansed to see your neighbors in their neediness, and you will be wise enough to love them according to the cry of their hearts.

> No one prays for himself, not even a hermit. He exists for others. . . . He belongs to everyone, and so he must share not only his food, but his thoughts, the graces that God may give him, and above all himself.
>
> — Catherine Doherty

They are hungry and thirsty, and we are not here to re-invent or re-create the gospel in any form except its pristine purity. Get yourself out of the way and let Jesus Christ, the Father, and the Spirit have dominion in every cell of your body.

The sum and substance of our life shows us that the deeper we go into our heart, where God lives, the more we are drawn by the Holy Spirit to go forth—whether it's to go to our next-door neighbor, to far away places, or to give the gospel to those who are hungry for love. We cannot be interiorized without going forth to give everything away. If anything is obvious, it is that we are apostles.

Catherine was able to see all of the elements of this culture of death that we're immersed in. No doubt this spiritual knowledge of the conflict that was facing the world penetrated her soul and moved her relentlessly to really take hold of the gospel in ordinary everyday life with such a passion—regardless of opposition, suffering, or darkness of faith. The insight that she had as to the malady of the Western world in particular, is a mirror image of the grace of the Little Flower's short life, and her spiritual insight into the fact that only love could pierce the darkness. At the World Mission Congress in Rome during the Jubilee year, the Little Flower and Catherine shared the same podium.

We are being challenged to bring life and truth, love and joy to everyone who comes through our doors. We have to absorb the gospel reality of those facets of the world that are trying to lead us away from God. All of us have to be missionaries. All of us have one tiny area, one tiny scope of reality where we too can be missionaries in the same way that the Little Flower was and in the way that Catherine has given us.

This path of living the gospel through various cultures, with persons of divergent backgrounds and personal histories that have no commonality, other than the Lord Jesus Christ, is going to be more and more a challenge. There is no answer to what faces us on a communal level, except to guard our hearts, guard our tongues and beg God for purification, so that we can be fitting temples of his presence. All of us need to be discreet with our tongues, especially.

It is no accident that this week in our readings, we have been drawn to St. James. Here is something that is applicable for all of us right now:

"Remember this, my dear brothers, everyone should be quick to listen, but slow to speak and slow to human anger. God's saving justice is never served by human anger, so do away with all impurities and remnants of evil. Humbly welcome the Word which has been planted in you and can save your souls.

"But you must do what the Word tells you and not just listen to it and deceive yourselves. Anyone who listens to the Word and takes no action, is like someone who looks at his own features in a mirror and once he has seen what he looks like, goes off and immediately forgets it. But anyone who looks steadily at the perfect law of freedom, and keeps to it, not listening and forgetting, but putting it into practice, will be blessed in every undertaking.

"Nobody who fails to keep a tight rein on the tongue, can claim to be religious. This is mere self-deception. That person's religion is worthless. Pure, unspoiled religion, in the eyes of God our Father, is this: coming to the help of orphans and widows in their hardships, and keeping one's self uncontaminated by the world."[1]

It would behoove all of us to read on through Chapters 2 and 3 of James. For communal living and laying down our lives for one another, St. James gives us pearls of wisdom and a path to cleansing and purifying our hearts that can never be exhausted. Whenever any communal or personal disunity or disruption occurs in our dealings with one another, we could

1. James 1:19–26

seek wise counsel, by re-reading alone, together, or in the poustinia these words of St. James.

There is a level of listening and bowing before one another that has to increase. We must pray and be sensitive to the cross that our brother or sister is carrying, at any given moment. We are very quick to bandy about words, not realizing that words can destroy, or words can build up. To have custody of our thoughts and custody of our tongue is the most excruciating discipline needed in living as a family.

And while we're talking about the Word, I hope everyone realizes what it means when you sit down to write a letter to anybody. It not only forces you to recollect your thoughts and to shape them into something understandable to another person, but you open your heart and give through those words to whoever you're sending that letter. Communication is vital. We talk with one another, we write, and we pass on what comes out of our own humanity, because everything we do is shot full of the Father, Son, and Holy Spirit.

The ingenuity of love, and acquiring a vocabulary of gospel love, are breathtaking. It's one thing to acquire these as a solitary individual, but it's something quite different being immersed daily in close living quarters and ongoing daily life, where you have no control over who you're going to be with. If we are to love one another without counting the cost, we have to be realistic in knowing that some of us will desire it but not be able to do it in the demanding way that's placed upon us.

All of us have a place in the mystical body of Christ. We have to be clear minded and pure of heart when determining ways of allowing everyone who passes through our blue doors to stay free to live in community or to seek other ways of living the gospel, after having been immersed within the heart of the family for a time.

It is only in time that we will, perhaps, see dimly what God is doing in and through each one of us today. You who have just received your *Pax Caritas* cross, or are wondering about many things, remember that love will slowly transform your fidelity into grace for others.

Our love and particular charism for supporting the priesthood, often in silence and hiddenness, is a given. Especially, now, we must surround priests with our prayer, love, and support. They need it. The times are not easy for any priest, especially in North America. They often experience loneliness, huge parishes, problematic situations from a culture that is no longer totally Christian and increasing secularized.

To fast and pray is one way we can extend our love toward them. To fast from food is relatively simple but perhaps this year we could fast from judgments. Can we fast from envy, jealousy, and anger, for the sake of our priests? It requires discipline and grace to do that.

It is the priest who disseminates the life of God through the Eucharist. It is the priest who plants the seed of Baptism and the life of Jesus in us. It is the priest who has a sacramental ability to forgive our sins as God forgives our sins. We must do all we can as lay people, to see that this power given to us by Jesus Christ, himself, is not diminished in any way in the days ahead.

When you see how many Christian groups have been empowered by the Holy Spirit to live the gospel in this day and age, you get a slight understanding of the magnitude and the incredible dimension of what it means to be a Christian.

> There are three ways of touching God: in the Blessed Sacrament; in deep faith and love for priests; and in our neighbor, especially our forgotten, lonely, hungry, thirsty, dispossessed neighbor.
>
> — Catherine Doherty

The laity must pray for confidence. Our role in the Church has to be buttressed by the confidence that Catherine, herself, gave to us. The Holy Father was quoted in *L'Osservatore Romano* as urging the bishops of France to get teams of priests and lay people to provide ongoing formation. The need is everywhere.

"In the towns and villages of your Dioceses, lay people are taking increasing responsibilities in ecclesial life. They are ready to take their part in evangelization; they provide services of catechesis, liturgical leadership, and preparation for the sacraments, spiritual assistance to the sick or to prisoners, and reflection and activities in many social contexts. To do this in a gospel spirit, they often ask you to help them acquire the necessary training. In your Dioceses, as Bishop Fihey pointed out in his regional report, many initiatives have been taken: at the diocesan level or even at the level of

groups of Dioceses, you organize formation courses sometimes lasting several years for persons called to take on
responsibilities; it is evident that the lay faithful are thus
equipped to fulfill as well as possible the functions you can
entrust to them."

Pray for all priests, wherever you are, because the massive
breakdown is hitting in two areas. One is in families and the
other is in the priesthood. We who have a freer rein with our
poverty, chastity, and obedience must uphold, support, and
pray for those who are central to the sacramental life and for
those who give life to the primary community in any culture
and in any civilization; that is, the family.

Pray for priests. The fate of the world in many ways is
dependant upon their holiness, their death to self, and their
sacrificial life. We, the laity, must uphold them with prayer,
fasting, and sacrifice. This can be done in humble ways, just
through living our daily life according to God's will. Our
Lady, through our consecration, will do the rest. If we want
the fullness of life, we must communally gather together in
heartfelt supplication for the priesthood. The sum and substance of our life is to love one another.

So, to pray for the priests, we the laity must really ask that
the fire of love come upon them so that through their presence, they will be mediators of love, for this family and for
the Church. They are called "shepherds," and it is their place
to lead us, the laity, into the fullness of life, so that we can be
apostles across the world, incarnating the gospel in every
nation.

The priest's blessing, as well as his presence among us, is a fountainhead of divine life. That flow of divinity doesn't stop with the priests, it only begins through, with, and by them, because this is how Jesus instituted the Church. It wasn't to dominate and control us, but to give us, in spite of the sinfulness or lack of faith of the priest himself, an everlasting fountain of life, truth, and love for each one of us.

We the laity are often lazy, and shut off that valve as soon as we leave Mass. Open up that valve and know that you are carriers and bearers of life for the whole world, in whatever corner of the family you serve. All too often we put things into little compartments.

Bless everyone and do not curse. Let us exercise blessings all day long, so that the face of Jesus Christ truly will overflow to all we meet, into the material world, and especially to our enemies. And let us see what happens in terms of the swelling of love among us.

We, the laity, teach by example. The word goes forth in printed materials, but the word is proclaimed from the rooftops in everything we do in and out of season, for work is prayer and prayer is work. Nothing that you touch, no matter how small, escapes the heart of love, himself.

We are in a revolution in biotechnology that is moving with such rapidity that what was once unthinkable, like cloning, is becoming more and more a reality. How does this world guide the development of new genetic knowledge and new biotechnologies so that they contribute to human flourishing, rather than create a world of stunted humanity, a world of souls without longing, without suffering, without surprises or desire? In a word, a world without love?

This advancement today in the explosion of scientific knowledge has put the globe into a catastrophic struggle, challenging the world in regard to life and death, love and hate, good and evil, as never before. It is because of this that the pressure of God's purification is upon each and every one of us. This is why the challenge of the cross has become so pressing. We can rejoice for we have made a decision for God, for love, for life, for the gospel. So we do not need to be afraid, we need to trust as never before, in our own personal lives and communally as an apostolate.

What we hear through the news media is usually very demoralizing. We have to guard our minds and our hearts so as to keep our eyes constantly focused on restoration and rebirth, and on finding that Jesus Christ is going to gather up all the fragments and bring forth something new. The fear and tension in society today comes because the old order is collapsing, and that will probably multiply and grow in the days

> The Church is called to bear witness to Christ by taking courageous and prophetic stands in the face of the corruption of political or economic power; by not seeking her own glory and material wealth; by using her resources to serve the poorest of the poor and by imitating Christ's own simplicity of life.
>
> — John Paul II,
> *Redemptoris Missio*

ahead. The irony of it all is that when you're traveling, through North America especially, everything looks wonderful, but the underbelly is not wonderful at all.

I forewarn you that because history is out of control, so are we. What we see today may be gone tomorrow, but the one thing we have is our love for one another, our unity, and the living presence of the living God in our hearts, beating strongly and more solidly in each of us, day by day. We have nothing to fear, for God is victorious and leading us into a resurrection, the like of which we cannot imagine.

To all of us who are being faced with cleansing, purification and a return to our Christian roots as never before, it is perfectly obvious that the hunger and desire for this is coming not merely from our own inner cry of the heart, but from the pressure of God himself upon us. Rejoice in this, for it means that grace is coming little by little. Everyone must help his neighbor and trust that God is working in and through his neighbor to reach the point when we no longer live but Christ lives in us.

Remember we have very little time. We must be ready, and we must be open to receive everything that God wants to give us, not only for our own salvation, but for the salvation of so many who are waiting in prison, in poverty, in bondages of addictions, in places where the faith has been watered down almost to extinction. Let us be that light which penetrates the darkness and violence that seems to be growing.

The following is an excerpt from a report sent by the director of our house in Russia. It reflects a great grace that came to the three staff workers there, and I pray you take it into your own heart for it is a forerunner of what God will ask of all of us.

"Alma had an incredible experience and a painful one during her two months of travel in central Russia and the Ukraine. Everywhere she found a spiritual desert. She experienced her poverty on every level and the only thing she had was *prayer*. She practiced obedience of a very humble sort, just doing what she was told like a little child. She came back knowing that she must willingly live here in Magadan[2] what she had lived on her journey. During this time, Miriam and I were being led more and more to the acceptance and the embracing of the cross. Somehow, in all this, obedience began to come to the fore. I felt a change in myself, a need to direct our apostolate more directly, if I could put it that way.

"About this time, our pastor seemed to be getting a word for us regarding obedience. A call to an obedience that was unhesitating and without argument. There was a sense of what happens in battle. The commanding officer speaks and the troops obey. That's it. We are now in a spiritual warfare so deep that, without that radical obedience, we are sunk. Then when he returned from Fatima, his word for us communally was: obedience without hesitation or questioning, and unity of mind and heart. I can't explain how but I immediately saw that *sobornost* and obedience are linked, and there will never be real *sobornost* without obedience. The icon of the Holy Trinity (by Rublev) flashed through my mind: the humble

2. Magadan is located in Siberia. It was the city through which those sent to the concentration camps passed.

inclination of the three angels to each other—no superior or inferior, yet a perfect harmony and obedience to the will of the Father."

We Westerners detest and abhor the word obedience, but all of us are being led to the cross of Jesus Christ and if we are not obedient even unto death we will not, cannot, get through the days that are coming very quickly upon the whole world.

The Siberian winter is very cold; 20 to 30 degrees below zero is common. You're never warm. You're never comfortable. You're never at ease but are constantly living on the edge of exquisite human discomfort. Yet never in all my travels have I experienced a depth of peace so palpable. For the first time in my life, I experienced there what it is to truly live in the heart of the Mother of God. *Peace, peace, and more peace.*

I beg the women of our apostolate to sacrifice and if possible to fast, and in your hearts to take your brothers to Mass every day and make an offering on their behalf before you receive the Eucharist. Let us lay down our lives with love, mercy, and tenderness for them.

Remember that men in our culture are being tempted by big things, by power, by technology, by sex. The men in our apostolate are also tempted by forces that mitigate against their taking the last place and laying down their lives in the extraordinary hiddenness and humility demanded by this vocation. We must love and serve them in silence and in hiddenness, in a way that will pierce the heavens and bring grace for us all. If we can come together as one in prayer to Our

Lady, and to the Father, the Son and the Spirit, I know in
faith that some tremendous gift will come to all of us.

We must pray for the grace to forgive each other so that
many, many people may be drawn to Christ through this
vocation.

We have a great spiritual heritage that has been given to us
through Catherine. Little did we realize that her gathering up
of the fragments of both East and West, and weaving them
into the very fabric of our daily life, would come into focus
so quickly.

The bishops from Eastern and Central Europe, at their
Synod, gave witness to the terrible martyrdom of so many
during the communistic persecution. For those martyrs and
for those faithful who lived through communism, the cele-
bration of the Eucharist, contemplation, and prayer were
their only links with Christ and the Church. These elements
are characteristic of Eastern Spirituality. Through them the
West has awakened to the Holy Father's prophetic statement,
his frequent reference to the Church's "two lungs," the
Church of the West and the Church of the East.

Archbishop Raya has given us a love for the Oriental
Liturgy, for the beauty of icons, for the richness of the Eastern
thrust that has come to all of us in such an awesome and tangible fashion. It is in our blood at this point, even though it
may not be quickly recognized, because most of us here are
Roman Catholic. It's as if a grafting has taken place in our
own history, whereby this fusion of East and West has slow-

ly taken form; and it is going to be even more prevalent in the years ahead.

A positive awareness of Western Europeans' faith did come through this gathering at the Synod. It highlighted the charism on the Liturgy, on prayer, on devotion to Mary, and on Christological formation. This particular Synod was given a vigorous thrust, from discouragement to new life.

We who stand still in our daily life can, without going across the world, pilgrim to any person who walks in the door. We pilgrim to our place of work. We become pilgrims, going to Mass every day. We can be pilgrims in a deep, deep, sense, taking with us our poverty, our trust, our dependence upon God for everything, and letting him strip us in silence and hiddenness, through the joys and pains of our daily life. All it really requires is a desire and a willingness to let go of everything, to let the Lord move us into meeting him.

Pray! Pray! Pray! Let us ask only one question. How can we love and serve and fill the growing hunger of souls every-where for the love, the mercy, and the tenderness of God and his Mother?

Chapter XI

Being Hopeful

"He has filled the starving with good things,
sent the rich away empty."

— Luke 1:53

Catherine said, "Perhaps we need to train our bodies, minds, and emotions to grow in courage, to shed fears, to grow in faith and love of God—a faith in love that humbly and simply prays:

'Lord I am ready to live and die for you,
and I accept whatever form of death
   that your will has selected for me—
but I am weak and my soul is housed in a house of sod.
Be my strength.
Give me but one gift, the gift of perfect love of you
   that casts out all fears.
If the death comes that you will for me,
and I have to do a last witnessing for you,
may I have the courage and the love
to witness joyfully, gladly, with a song in my soul
and with full control over my limbs, my face,
   and my mind."[1]

The Holy Father began his pontificate with the words, "Be not afraid." It is seldom, wherever he appears, regardless of whom he's addressing, regardless of the continent which he is visiting, that he does not repeat these words to the multitudes that gather to hear him. Be not afraid! Be not afraid!

Christians today need to listen to this voice that brings light and hope and peace and love wherever he goes. It is awesome to see how one man, now enfeebled, struggling

1. Catherine Doherty, "The Various Faces of Courage, July 26, 1958." In *Dearly Beloved: Letters to the Children of My Spirit, Volume One.* Rev. ed. (Combermere ON: Madonna House Publications, 1989), 72.

with physical suffering, does not lose his impact upon those he addresses. As a matter of fact, it seems as though the radiance of the presence of God increases in him and is shedding its rays of faith, hope, and love across the whole globe.

Never has there been a pontificate that has been persecuted with more vehemence than this one. The Holy Father has many, many enemies. I was struck by one thought. Through the years he has stood firm in the face of conflict, yet leaned toward the little people. His persistent writing of encyclicals, his unceasing visits to countries across the world, and his unflinching vision of the gospel will lead the Church through this new millennium of Christendom. That alone gives us hope and assurance that the vault of heaven is opening wide.

This is a man with a supreme spiritual authority for all Christians. So I say, be not afraid whenever you face a challenge of any kind, but take hold of the Word of God with the assurance of your heritage. Go quickly to Scripture or pray to the Holy Spirit to give you a reminder of what you need at this time. If you are tempted by anything, by your own confusing thoughts or doubts, or by discouragement, go to the power of the Word of God and reinforce your mind.

What must we pray for together at this time? We must pray for hope.

We live in faith. We realize that our faith needs to be rooted in daily life and buttressed by prayer, loving service, and fidelity. As a body, though, this is the time for corporate hope.

Individually and together, we are climbing the mountain of the Lord. Search the purgations that St. John of the Cross and St. Teresa of Avila wrote about. The desire to live in God and have God live in us, to be united only in the love of God has grown into a fire that you can touch, taste, and see. A tangible strength is moving in and through us.

This is what the Catechism of the Catholic Church says about hope:

"The virtue of hope responds to the aspiration to happiness which God has placed in the heart of every man; it takes up the hopes that inspire men's activities and purifies them so as to order them to the Kingdom of God; it keeps man from discouragement; it sustains him during times of abandonment; it opens up his heart in the expectation of eternal beatitude. Buoyed up by hope, he is preserved from selfishness and lead to the happiness that flows from charity."[2]

"Hope is a weapon that protects us in the struggle of salvation. 'Let us put on the breastplate of faith and charity and for a helmet, the hope of salvation.'[3] It affords us joy, even under trial. 'Rejoice in your hope, be patient in tribulation.'[4] Hope is expressed and nourished in prayer, especially in the Our Father, the summary of everything that hope leads us to desire."[5]

Are we ready? Are we alert to meet whatever tomorrow brings? Do we have true poverty, true chastity, and true obedience? Our promises to live these three have no meaning unless they are under the Spirit of God and are ordered to the duty of the moment.

Be not afraid of whatever pain the Spirit probes in your heart today. Have gratitude for everything and offer the chalice of your being, body, mind, heart and soul to the Father

2. *Catechism of the Catholic Church* (Vatican: Liberia Editrice Vaticana, 1994), 1818.

3. Ephesians 6:14

4. Romans 12:12

5. *Catechism of the Catholic Church*, 1820.

each morning. Then our communal surrender will be mobilized more quickly into a union of mind and heart, to help the Church and our Lord pour forth his mercy upon a world in need. Drink deeply of the beatitudes and be obedient to your Lord Jesus by staying faithful to everything he asks.

Yesterday the little sign "Nazareth" leaped out from its place on the side of the poustinia. This morning I turned to Catherine's words from the history of our Apostolate:

"To me Nazareth also meant (besides the life of poverty) simplicity, peace and love—the antithesis of the complex European-American-Canadian societies I observed in Toronto and other big cities on the North American continent, and of which I was very tired. A new civilization was being born in the twenties, after World War I, and the rat race we know so well now in the sixties was really beginning to be felt. In these American centers conformity was evident, as were a constantly growing materialism, and the breakdown of the family, as well as the breaking up of old traditions. There was little peace. Somehow I wanted to get away from all this, and restore and preserve what was good in the past. I tied it up with religion in my mind—

> *Faith allows us to enter peacefully into the dark night which each of us faces at one time or another. Faith walks simply, like a child, between the darkness of human life and the hope of what is to come, "for eye has not seen, nor ear heard what God reserves for those who love him." Faith is a kind of folly, the folly that belongs to God himself.*
>
> — Catherine Doherty

with the Liturgy, and with the peace of God, purchased through the works of one's hands and not only of one's brains."[6]

The mystery born in our obscure village is slowly taking shape in the heart of Our Lady of the Trinity. The challenge of the Holy Father to create a culture of life is truly being fleshed out here. The radical dimension of Nazareth is the hope of a new civilization.

We are certainly at the end of an era. You can be sure that the entire world, the Church, and all mankind are stepping onto a bridge. There is no turning back! What has been a cultural and historical reality is reaching a climax. The old order is dead and no one can see clearly how nations, people, and cultures will deal with cataclysmic changes.

We're called to restore all things to Christ. The unfolding of history, that is, of our own errors, has to be seen from the perspective of the gospel.

We often hear the pros and cons about the technological progress that is upon us. The rapidness of change makes it urgent that we wrestle with all of these things. Everyone ponders e-mails, faxes, videos, cassettes, and certainly the computer with serious prayer and much communication. We

---

6. Catherine Doherty, "Background for Spiritual Formation." Chap. 3 in *The History of the Apostolate of Friendship House and Madonna House* (unpublished).

have to look at this constantly so that we are not dehumanized nor pulled away from the essence of our life, which is to love God and to love one another. This acceleration is going to require greater prayer, pondering, and communication.

Technology is a tool. It will affect every aspect of human society. It behooves us to keep abreast with what the Church says regarding this, for Christians. At the same time, we must know that there is a great good coming out of everything, to deflect and offset what can potentially be an instrument for isolation, dehumanization, and death.

We belong to and are dedicated to the culture of life. We have to jump into this stream and use all the means of restoration with confidence and courage. But don't fool yourself. You have to wrestle with these elements in every possible way. We're able to maintain the glory of being truly human for the sake of others in a fashion that many parts of society would find difficult. Loneliness, isolation, and materialism are certainly factors that hit very hard at the core of the human heart. Let us not see anything as being a detriment to the Christian faith. It's a question of how do we use everything on this earth for the greater glory of God, in time and in eternity.

We are in the 21st century, but in a way, the Christian body is just beginning to grasp and see what it is that God has done for us. None of us want a theoretical God. None of us want to know about God. All of us want to know God! We want to have him be our lover, and we want more than anything to love him back, no matter what the cost. There is an urge and a desire and a hunger that is becoming more insatiable all the time. We can be grateful and give thanks for the fact that this awakening is becoming more adamant day by day.

At the time of Christ, the Roman Empire was at its zenith. The Roman genius held together massive amounts of people and land by sustaining its communication through interlocking roads. At the time of our Lord's birth, he entered into this civilization and preached the good news. Twelve men were the first apostles. After Pentecost, the fire and flame of the gospel spread rapidly across these roads, and the beginning of the Church took place.

Today, because of the Internet, the communication system is reaching its tentacles across the world. Could it be in the mind of the Father that this could be used in such a way that the gospel, the fire of the Word, can be proclaimed, when and if we have to enter the catacombs? It is only a question to ponder and to pray about for the future.

As you know, Catherine had a holy fear of technology because it is such a powerful tool. It is, however, just that—a tool, which means it can be used for good. At the same time it calls us to a greater fidelity to the little things, to person-to-person contact, and to restoration, by natural means, of the earth and all God's gifts to his creatures through his abundant creation. All things work for good for those who love God. The extremes of being able to communicate instantly with people all over the world, and at the same time of knowing our limitations as creatures, are breathtaking.

The greatest gift is the presence of Jesus Christ living uniquely in each one of us. It is not what we do that matters but what he does in and through us.

Interiorization will be the greatest gift and the greatest protection for incarnating the gospel that all of us are going to
have. If we are interiorized so that we believe, know, and
trust that the living God is walking with us, talking through
us, and being an emanation of love and peace wherever we
go, then we can handle and move with whatever is going to
transpire in the next few years.

I can't repeat enough that history is out of control and we
have no idea what will happen in the new millennium. The
Church may bloom, be reborn and revitalized, and overcome
this mounting culture of death that is all around us. On the
other hand, since history typically unfolds quietly and slowly, it may take 100 years. *We don't know!*

The culture of death is marching across the world with no
indication of repentance, which means that we, who have
laid our lives down for the gospel of Jesus Christ, must grow
in trust and confidence. Humility, littleness, and hiddenness
are the only weapons we will have in the days ahead. Fear is
being trampled down and life is coming.

The world is being offered a dramatic choice more and more
clearly as each day unfolds. Will we, one by one, choose life
or death? Will we choose to love or to close our hearts to our
fellowmen? Will we choose to say, "I will" or will we enclose
ourselves in the prisons of fear, smallness of heart, and selfishness? Let us pray that each of us, through the little things
that face us day by day, can be brought into the Triumph of
the Holy Cross. If God himself has poured his life out for us
and continues to watch over each of us, who can say, "It is not
possible"? Our God is alive.

Let us rejoice and be glad. At the same time, let us grow very small and very, very secure in the heart of our Lord and his Mother. We know in faith that anything good that comes from any one of us is a sheer gift of their great love, mercy, and steadfastness.

Let us pray for a happiness that our Lord wants to give us. Let us ask Our Lady to give us the capacity to surrender as she did two thousand years ago. Let us trust that we, the children of this culture, have been chosen to stand as a burning bush before the forces that want to deny the resurrection. Let us rejoice that our heritage is to have the fullness of life while standing still in the ordinariness of today.

We are now, as a body, at least like little fledglings, up on our feet. And so we must bow toward one another in love and respect, listening and laying down our lives for one another in a new dimension. We have to keep doing this until all of us can say, "I no longer live, but Christ lives in me."[7]

We must always remember that this movement of the Holy Spirit to create the family of God in the midst of a society as broken as our own, can only be designed to be a major sign of contradiction.

7. Galatians 2:20

Time is short and the budding signs of a growing confrontation between spiritual forces is everywhere. All you have to do is pick up a newspaper or a magazine, or see current movies and television programs to read the signs of the time. You'll find pornography, euthanasia, murder by abortion, children trying to blow up schools, nations being ripped to pieces by internal wars. On the other hand, for those who stand for life, love, God, there is an overwhelming revival. Witness the profusion of Catholic periodicals that have been launched just within the last ten to fifteen years. There is a mind-boggling diet of good Catholic periodicals, mostly put out by lay people.

We are in a catastrophe and we know the outcome, but that outcome can be delayed, short circuited, or watered down to the degree of the fire in your heart and mine.

Many within our own family are undergoing enormous transforming purifications. Many face pain or unspeakable fears. But all of that can be transcended, because God's presence is coming to you every day that you're faithful to the duty of the moment and every day that you receive the living Lord in the Eucharist.

We don't have a minute to lose. Give your life to others. Pray and see how you can truly be the hands, the feet, the eyes, the ears, the heart of Jesus Christ, whether you're in the Yukon, the Caribbean, Europe, Brazil, Ghana, or in the kitchen in Combermere. Wherever you are, you carry God, and someone is waiting to receive the love he gives you today, to pass through you to those who are desperate for a drop of living water.

In the days ahead if we are to face possible martyrdom, be it white or red, let us be prepared. Pray for one another and cling, cling with all your might to life, the life that comes from God.

*W*e all must watch the signs of the times, without fear, and with faith in who we are as a Christian body. The two words we must cling to are unity and love. We have to be united in everything, not according to human thinking, but in the heart of Jesus Christ. These are momentous times and it is imperative that we fear nothing, and cling to the duty of the moment and to our faith.

> Everything can be borne between two Masses. When you eat the bread of heaven, you will be able to face any kind of day. . . . You will plunge into the sea of fire that is the Mass and come out burning, ready to go forth and light fires of love.
>
> — Catherine Doherty

Look back and see how Blessed John XXIII opened the windows of the Church with Vatican II. He let in fresh air! Now we've learned that he is an incorruptible! What a magnificent sign of the times this is. When life is being thrown out through abortion and euthanasia and other means, Pope John the Good comes forth as a visible sign of the power of the Eucharist, of the Incarnation, to challenge this world.

Then came Pope Paul VI who threw his body over a bleeding, fragmented, divided Church, when it appeared that the whole Church might be splintered into many factions. We, who lived through that era, know that it was indeed a very difficult period in Christian history.

Now we have John Paul II who, according to Catherine, relieved her of the burden of carrying the Church. She knew that we now had a Father of the faith, *who would gather up the fragments lest they be lost.* He is doing that not only for the Christian body; his fatherly love bends to the Jews, the Hindus, the Buddhists, to all men of good will.

No matter where you are, no matter what you do, the living God lives in you and we have nothing to fear, for a blaze of glory and light comes out of every man and woman, every priest, quietly, silently, and hiddenly. Nothing will overcome a Christian. Nothing can destroy a Christian.

Trust that at this moment, individually and communally, God's hand is upon us and that he's simply saying, "Come higher, friend."

When the Holy Spirit begins to move not just one of us, but all of us, a disturbance begins. We will come up against drifting parts of our inner life—perhaps we've become complacent or self-directed, or been tempted by mediocrity. Let us never allow that to happen. Let us throw our life away and jump into the abyss of faith knowing that Almighty God is there to catch us. We can never give in to mediocrity, because we've come out of the heart of God, and we constantly return to the merciful, all-living, fiery presence of the Trinity within us, around us, piercing hidden corners everywhere.

Be grateful for any struggle, be grateful for anything that jars your sensibilities. Do not say, "What have I done wrong?" Simply look, like a child, toward Our Lady and her Son and say to Jesus Christ, "What are you trying to give me?" "What are you trying to teach me?" "I am ready." Surrender each day with a totality of childlike trust and confidence, and nothing will stop us from receiving more joy, love, and fullness of life.

More and more we see that we are receiving the blessings of God through the universal Church, especially from John Paul II. Keeping our vision wide and deep will protect us from the attacks against the Church taking place, especially in the Western world. All of these attacks will be overcome, for it was Jesus Christ who laid the foundation through Peter and nothing will rock or destroy that foundation. Catherine's vision has taken us back in a contemporary way to the Fathers of the Church. So our daily life rooted in trust and faith, in prayer and the duty of the moment, will build in silence and hiddenness what can never be destroyed: *love*.

> "By her manifold intercession she (the Mother of God) continues to obtain for us the graces of eternal salvation. By her maternal charity, she takes care of the brethren of her Son who still journey on earth surrounded by dangers and difficulties, until they are led into their blessed home." (The Second Vatican Council)
>
> — John Paul II, *Dives In Misericordia*

To say that we do not feel the tensions of the forces of darkness and light still at our elbow would be an untruth, but we know in faith that Jesus Christ, present today, tomorrow, and forever, is in us, with us, and leading us into this third millennium. We are following with childlike hearts, grateful for having been chosen to be a part of this great event.

Several persons have said that in time to come, people will marvel at those who lived through the '90s, when it appeared as though death was going to be victorious over life. Well, the spiritual leaders of the world have pushed through the Holy Doors and we know that our Redeemer lives and there is nothing to fear. Let us be bold in the days ahead and choose life and love, and fear nothing, for the living God lives in us.

We must pray for one another as never before and we must love one another with total acceptance, in tenderness and in hope.

God is raising up an army of saints all over the world. We must break open the smallness of our mediocrity, complacency, and narrow vision; and drink from the wellspring of life and love wherever the Holy Spirit draws us. The whole world is groaning and moving toward rebirth, in the Church and in our Christian heritage. God himself is smashing the human sin, personally and collectively. We must keep our eyes on truth and love.

Two young men who were with us for our pre-seminarian program endeared themselves to us. One has rosy cheeks and bright, sparkling eyes. He has always been a model of youthful maturity, to put it in simple language. The other one arrived more of a challenge to the entire family. He had a tendency to try to skip out of common chores. For a time, it looked as though he might not make it here, but with a little encouragement and a wee bit of a correction here and there, he settled down. He became a sterling, prayerful, and ardent young man. The two of them recently returned for a visit.

They were like the face of hope arriving, because they had just spent four months pilgrimaging to holy places in Europe. They did not go by modern convenience or as bourgeois tourists would go. They went as pilgrims, knocking at monastery doors for lodging, seeking their meals from whoever would feed them, carrying with them a sleeping bag in the event that there was no bed for them.

These two young men prayed their way through Europe and walked or hitchhiked from place to place. They had story after story of how exceedingly well cared for they were throughout the entire trip. They carried nothing with them except one change of clothing so their backpacks wouldn't encumber them.

The highlight of their pilgrimage was meeting a grand, elderly man in Rome. Although they had no connections in the higher echelons, they were standing in St. Peter's Square on the eve of the opening of the Holy Doors. A woman walked up to them and said, "Would you like two tickets for St. Peter's?" They were escorted to a place in the Basilica not far from the Holy Father at that momentous time when John Paul II led the Church into the third millennium.

As they told their story, it was as though they took us all with them, because they have a great love for Madonna House and radiate the hunger and thirst that is so unquenchable in the hearts of young people like them. When they left the other morning, it was as though a ray of sunshine left with them.

Pray for all these young people who carry within them the future of the Church and the future of the world, whether they live out their life as married people, as lay people in the marketplace, or as priests or nuns. Whatever path they take, they will be the hands, hearts, and instruments whereby restoration will come for future generations. We thank them for coming.

These two young men are symbols of this surge of life all around us. What an honor it is to receive them into our home and our hearts. What an incredible grace it is for us to pass on to them whatever incarnation of the gospel is placed in our hands, in whatever corner of the Apostolate we are living and serving in. I pray that we pass it on with fire in our hearts, because love is the only thing that can never be extinguished from the face of the earth.

All of us are called to be missionaries, which means to become an icon of Christ.

It is a time to look up, with expectant hope as never before, and to rejoice in our poverty, weakness, even sinfulness. We have the greatest riches of all, the presence of the living God, constantly bubbling up with joy and fire in every one of our hearts.

C h a p t e r   X I I

A New Springtime

*"He has come to the help of Israel
his servant, mindful of his faithful love—
according to the promise he made to our
ancestors—of his mercy to Abraham
and to his descendants forever."*

— Luke 1:54–55

Come, Lord Jesus!
Come and live in us.
Come, Lord Jesus!
Gather together the fragments of the earth.
Bring all the nations into your heart now.
Lord Jesus,
bring all of the baptized back together
into one body.
We all hunger for that.

Father Briere once encapsulated the intellectual awareness of the anticipated demise of Western civilization. He pointed out that in the '30s, long before anyone thought of the catastrophe, several books were published independently of one another that came to be known as "crisis literature." Many authors including Maritain, Guardini, Sorokin, Peter Watts, Belloc, and Berdyaev, in one way or another, came to similar conclusions. They said that we have reached the end of an historical era and are entering into another one, but the transition between the two will be catastrophic.

The '70s were the heart of this transition, a most confused time. A Tower of Babel was built and remains among intellectuals, economists, politicians, and leaders of nations. People do not listen to and cannot communicate with one another. After this terrible confusion, according to Father's assessment of the writings, mankind will rise to a higher degree of spirituality, a flowering of spirituality. We now pray that this flowering will be the fulfillment of Our Lady's promise and triumph, as well as the constancy in which the Holy Father points to the millennium.

Catherine spiritually warned us and prepared us for this flowering. She simply and clearly said that we must take Scripture and put those words into practice. To merely hear the Word and not do it, will get us nowhere.

The Little Mandate must sing in our hearts. Each one of us has to take these words and incarnate them in whatever marketplace we serve, be it Russia, Arizona, our gift shop, farm, kitchen, or Washington. Love dwells everywhere. Our response in doing little things well for the love of God is the only response we can have to this catastrophe that is all over the world.

We were all shaken to the core by the terrorist attack on the World Trade Center in New York. When we gathered for our staff meeting, we read "Confrontation with Evil and Martyrdom" from *Poustinia*. We felt an urgency to take hold of Catherine's words "stand still."

All of us should read the chapters "Repent" and "Wars and Rumors of Wars" from her book *Urodivoi*, as well. It makes you shudder to see how prophetic these words are for the times we're living through.

Catherine was a voice for God. We her children need to take her writings seriously. We have entered a new era. The world as we knew it before September 11th, 2001, is finished. Only God knows what is coming. But we can trust that God's mercy is on its way, even if pockets of uncertainty, challenge, fear, and disruption flow for a period of time. We know in faith that God is reclaiming his earth and all of his children.

We need to keep our Christian perspective. When the Barbarian hordes cascaded across Europe at the time of St.

Augustine, he calmly wrote his famous work, *City of God*. Nations rise and fall, civilizations come and go, but Jesus Christ, Son of the Living God, has been given to us. Eventually, he will draw all men and all nations to himself. When you feel threatened go and find your hope in the Word. More than anything, remember that Jesus Christ, through your baptism, has entered into your pain and nothing can ever overcome his love.

The Holy Father repeatedly talks about the Springtime in the Church coming in the third millennium. Looking at the world, it seems impossible to turn today's overwhelming thrust against life into a refurbished and glorified time in the history of the Church. But we know that light is coming faster and faster.

> It would be foolish to try to restore the world en masse. We must begin to restore it person by person.
>
> — Catherine Doherty

Let us stand erect and strong and hold hands with all our brothers and sisters wherever we are, and know that the darkness has already been broken because the word has gone forth that Our Lady is going to be victorious. Let us rejoice and be glad and give thanks for this wonderful era that we are living in, whereby the future is assured, for every word will be fulfilled that was spoken by Jesus Christ when he walked the earth 2,000 years ago.

Our Lady brings each of us here to Madonna House. Not for herself, but to lead each of these young people and all of us into the heart of the Trinity. This life is extraordinary when what we do is humble and simple, hidden and ordinary. We see reflected in the people who come to us and in the way people are graced here that the interior journey that each one of us is on is far beyond what any of us can even begin to understand.

Many old religious communities are floundering and some will die, but new movements are proliferating, worldwide. We are perhaps one of the oldest new communities, at least in the Western world. Our vocation is also by far the most difficult to incarnate, so we are the slowest to show the fruit of our dedication. Don't get discouraged! It's coming folks, because people are taking this life seriously.

Walking from place to place has provided a powerful reminder of the incarnation happening. In the dining room yesterday morning the vitality and the concentrated presence to one another was very striking. It didn't mean that there weren't burdens and pain in people, but it is as though new life is coming.

The music, the exuberance of our guests, who are remarkable young men and women, give us hope. They're eager and hungry to absorb the ordinary demands of our hidden and seemingly unexciting life. You can sense a deep invisible vibrancy running like a thread here, there, and everywhere.

I see beauty and tenderness in every corner of our house. This blesses all of us. This protects us and gives us shelter, to let the Lord grow in us with his Father and the Spirit.

I send these words simply because they also reflect what the Holy Father says about the new Springtime. It gives us courage, even though there may be difficult days ahead, to unify our individual pains with Christ for the salvation of souls and to rest in the assurance of the ultimate glory of the cross. This is a great gift in our hidden life of Nazareth. We need not fear anything, because we're walking, and some of us are running, to the expectant rebirth of Christianity and of this poor, poor world that is so beset by misery.

This is the time for us to stop, look, and listen. Receive everything as a sheer gift from God, whether it be joy or sorrow, a chastisement or a consolation. It doesn't matter, as long as we, like little children, take everything as being a gift of God for each of us personally, and for the whole family.

We must keep our eyes on the civilization of love. We must keep our eyes on creating a great human and spiritual way of life. We must be one with our Lord and his Mother in creating little corners of new life, of beauty, of tenderness. We must let our hands touch all the material things that come through our houses with reverence and respect. We must see them as tools and gifts of restoration.

> Now I point to Mary once again as the radiant dawn and sure guide for our steps. Once more, echoing the words of Jesus himself and giving voice to the filial affection of the whole Church, I say to her: Woman, behold your children. (John 19:26)
>
> — John Paul II,
> *Novo Millennio Ineunte*

All things are being passed through the mind and heart of God so that we, his children, can be restored for the birth into a new civilization of love, into something far more beautiful than we can hope for or imagine, for the whole world. Pass it on, whatever you have that brings goodness, truth, beauty, and love for others. Pass it on.

There is a different breed of young people coming here. They are post-Vatican II children. Many of them have been raised by "Charismatic" parents. Many have had quite unusual experiences of God, himself. Many have converted, in spite of parents who do not practice the faith. They are being touched directly by God in one way or another. They are bright, alert, hungry, and a joy to have in this house. They are the future and it is obvious that something is unfolding in a most positive fashion.

We must enter into their hearts and listen to them and listen to the heartbeat of God in them, because they are the ones who will have to do the reconstruction and the restoration. We have a certain wisdom of experience, living in community life. They have a freshness and an expression of life.

Both generations must come together and harmonize in a new way. They are a magnificent challenge and it bodes well, not only for future vocations, but also for restoration of Christendom wherever they may be. Nothing, nothing can stop the ongoing incarnation of the gospel.

Rome is paying a lot of attention to the new lay movements. They are urging us to get tied into the universal Church more solidly, so that the temptation to exclusivity will be avoided. It is one of the things that we, too, have to be constantly aware of in this age when the Holy Spirit seems to be pressing upon all Christians to bring forth a new Springtime.

This vision of a new civilization is the most realistic part of our life. It echoes what the Holy Father calls a Springtime in the church. Our small but important contribution to this aspect of a restored church comes from our love for one another. We have been practicing through the nitty-gritty of everyday life for years and years and years.

Be bold! Have confidence! Stand rooted in our heritage. Safeguard it. Pass it on with generous hearts. The world is starving for life, love, and truth. We have these in our way of life, but our life will die if we do not pass them on. Let us run, not walk, into the third millennium, going deeper and higher into the gospel.

Do you want to be a disciple of Jesus Christ? Then pray to be disciplined.

Do you want to be a fire, a flame? Then do violence only to yourself.

Do you want to live in the truth, and do you want fulfillment? Then stop looking at the secular world and its egocentric, selfish, me-centered reality and begin to practice, to incarnate, to exercise in your daily life the words of Jesus Christ.

Do you want your "rights"? Do you want justice? Do you want to be a person? Then die and leave your rights at the doorstep. The only right we have is to sacrifice our whole life for the sake of the kingdom.

Do you want to live with childlike simplicity and know a peace, a joy, an inner reality that no one can take from you? Then wash your mind in the truth of Jesus Christ, discipline your reactions to your brothers and sisters, submit any request that comes your way to these criteria:

What is Jesus Christ offering me at this moment?

What is he saying to me at this moment?

What is he trying to give me at this moment?

When we're being purified or stripped, the pain and the discouragement sometimes are so enormous that we will do anything to run from them. There's no turning back once you have been hooked by the "Hound of Heaven," by love himself. Pain is the kiss of Christ. We must grasp this.

We've been growing in this awareness. Now it is going to get deeper. We're entering a new era on a spiritual level. There are signs of the Springtime of the Church in every corner. No matter where you are in this transforming power of love, just let God do with you what he will. He will do the work and all you have to do is say "Yes" to it and resound with a fervent "Thank you" for everything that happens each day. We have learned that we can judge no one, that we can change no one but ourselves, that we are powerless before one another, and that we have to let go of expectations of one another. Deepen that commitment at this hour and at this time in history.

Pray daily for the fire of God's love to ignite your heart. Pray daily for the gift of faith. Pray daily that what God has ordained for us will become a living reality. "He who gives up his life will find it,"[1] does not mean death in the way that we view it. It means emptying our own inner being of all that is broken, wounded, and sinful, so that the mercy of God can fill it. *He wants more than anything on this earth to give you the abundance of his love, mercy, and tenderness.*

Those who have chosen to stay faithful to their Christian heritage are being given a new life.

When the Holy Father began to speak, his hand was trembling and his body carried an obvious burden of physical suffering, but his words were powerful and penetrating, and his spirit was radiantly alive as he delivered a life-giving message. As he spoke, I thought that this is probably the greatest pope in history. He has come through the darkest era of history, suffering persecution, rejection, vilification, opposition on all sides—especially from consecrated priests and Sisters who ignored his spiritual authority.

John Paul II, this extraordinary pope, has given voice to the gospel and lifted us up in the most transcendent way. When he speaks, we don't think in terms of right or left, but we are enfolded in the truth of Jesus Christ. He doesn't hesi-

1. Matthew 10:39

tate to reach out and touch people, directly. People who are handicapped, victims of paralysis, or confined to a partial life, wheelchairs, or crutches, are the people he goes to. He seems to have a special love and tenderness toward them. The children, too, he gravitates toward with the love of a father. Just to see him move through a crowd is enough to make you weep with joy that we have such a father leading and guiding us into the new era, the new Springtime of the Church.

> Faith sees God's face in every human face.
>
> — Catherine Doherty

The new Springtime is already taking root in the midst of the tottering and crumbling old order of Western civilization, of Russia, and of the entire globe. Every nation is being challenged spiritually and materially, for we have to become brothers and sisters walking hand in hand or we will not be survivors.

As little, poor, humble, and simple as we are, we can join hands with the Holy Father and with the whole universal Church and give a resounding yes, so that we can live in love and in truth, so that we can live and spend our lives bringing love, truth, peace, and joy to everyone we meet.

E p i l o g u e

I want to conclude this little book by giving the last word to our founders: Catherine Doherty, Eddie Doherty and Father Callahan, whose faith and total dedication have given life to countless thousands of seekers.

Catherine says: "On the Feast of Our Lady's Purification, February 2nd, 1951, I finished a long journey. My journey ended at the feet of Our Lady's altar, in the church of the Sacred Heart in Ottawa, Canada, where my husband, Eddie Doherty, and I consecrated ourselves to Jesus through Mary, according to the true devotion of St. Louis de Montfort.[1] On that day, we handed over to her all of ourselves, our earthly goods, our spiritual merits, and good works, for her to do with as she pleases from now until our deaths. We became totally hers that lovely day.

"We walked out of the church as if we were walking on air. It was so nice to be utterly poor, and better still, to know that the little we had possessed was all hers.

"I came across Montfort several times along that journey of mine. Each time I turned away from him and from his true devotion, for both strangely repelled me. I definitely did not like the word 'slave.' So many people don't. And I did not like his old fashioned language, even though I read his book both in French and in English.

"Then again, I was busy, very busy, founding Friendship House (our first apostolate) and working among the forgot-

---

1. See St. Louis de Montfort, *True Devotion to Mary.* Adapted by Eddie Doherty. (Bayshore NY: Montfort Publications, 1956)

ten, the despised, and the poor in the alleyways and byways of the world. I was busy trying to learn to pray, to be before God before doing for God, lest I and my spiritual children should become guilty of the heresy of good works.

"I looked for some time for a basis on which to found my apostolic work. Slowly, my heart, soul, and mind turned to my old devotion, the hidden life of Christ, the Holy Family. That would be the answer. We would pattern our life on the humble, ordinary life of the Holy Family.

"This led me to Mary, the *Bogoroditza* as she is called in Russian. I loved her greatly, always turned to her. Now, the Holy Spirit, her Spouse, began to reveal her to me in a special way.

"Years went by; the journey went on. More lessons were given, learned, and integrated into our works of charity. Then I met a son of Montfort. He spoke to me of the true devotion. I listened respectfully, took his book, and read it slowly.

"But I laid the whole idea aside again. I did not feel any revulsion this time against the word 'slave,' for I had learned of the slavery of sin. It was all around me, sharply delineated and outlined. But what had I to offer the gracious Queen of Heaven that I had not yet given away? Worldly goods? I had none. Inner detachment from them? I had been working so long on that spiritual angle that it seemed little to offer. My body? That was given over to the service of her Son long ago. My merits? How small they were! So the true devotion was laid aside and gathered dust on my shelves. The journey went on.

"My son was in World War II. I had dedicated him in his infancy to Our Blessed Lady. I re-dedicated him, asking her to keep him safe. She did. If at all possible, my love for her grew and grew.

"On August 15, 1945, the feast of Our Lady's Assumption, the idea of an apostolate in Combermere, Ontario, was conceived. Two years later Eddie and I came to Combermere, a tiny village on the edge of nowhere. We devoted ourselves to the rural apostolate.

"This was the beginning of Madonna House, with its door painted blue in Mary's honor. It was her house, and she became co-foundress of this new apostolate of ours."[2]

Father Callahan, who became the founder of the priests, gave Madonna House the gift of the consecration. We often take this blessing for granted now, but it was a radical and rather revolutionary step when first introduced. Being Russian, Catherine was not immediately drawn to this form of devotion. Yet, when she and Eddie made this consecration, her "mystical life" leaped forward.

Blanche Lepinski, one of our closest friends and neighbors, and a former Friendship House staff member, says that the difference between Friendship House and Madonna House was the consecration. To her mind it thrust Madonna House into spiritual depths of faith, hope, and love that were deeper than anything known in Friendship House. It did not take away from the work but deepened the apostolate, which seemed to be on a firmer foundation.

We must be patient and trusting that God is forming us. Without a total and complete surrender to Our Lord through Our Lady, it cannot come to fruition. As long as we place our entire lives in her hands, nothing will stop the living out of the gospel according to the mind and heart of the foundress.

Catherine recounted the first anniversary of her consecration in her diary: "Today is the great day of the renewal of

2. Catherine Doherty, Staff Letter #128, February 23, 1999 (unpublished).

Eddie's and my slavery promises to Mary in the true devotion. Also it is the first day of my vow of poverty.

"It is a gray, rainy day. There is no sensible devotion about it. None. Yet with all my heart, mind, soul, and will, I give God the Father, through Jesus, through Mary, my life, my all, through the true devotion and the vow of poverty. Oh Maria, Mother and Queen, help me now to live both to the hilt, in their outward and inner meaning!

"Beloved, the sense of utter dedication through my promises, via the true devotion of Montfort to the Blessed Virgin, plus my vow of poverty, is still but a seed lying in frozen ground. It is there, of this I am conscious in joy, that I know that the heat of spring's charity must thaw the ground and water the seed."[3]

These words are very simple. Eddie and the Catherine's consecrations were done in the midst of many, many demands in their daily lives. We live in the marketplace, no matter where we are. Our door of hospitality must always be open, and our interruptions must become our work. There is no controlling our days. There is no controlling who will enter into our lives, moment by moment. But for all of us, this abandonment and yielding to whatever comes, both in joy and pain, is our on-going formation until the day we die.

Yes, we may gain greater clarity as the years pass. Certainly, we have greater communal wisdom. We have certain moments of discernment—we recognize when a corner of the house needs straightening, or when something taking place around us or within the fabric of family life is amiss. We've gained some capacity to read the signs of God. But this is simply an outer reordering—discarding habits, attitudes, and possessions that distract us, following a consecrated life of discipline, charity, and obedience that facilitates the call we

3. Cf. Catherine's diary, February 2, 1952, and Staff Letter #106, July 28, 1999 (unpublished).

share to enter into a new and deeper relationship with God himself.

In faith we know that life, that seed that was planted when we first made our consecration to Our Lady, is growing in each according to their life experience, into a greater flowering of this mystery of love.

The poverty of Jesus became evident when he allowed himself to be conceived in the womb of a woman. If our poverty comes anywhere near that poverty, we will be rich indeed. This mystery of faith that restores and refashions us is so far beyond our intellects and ideas that we have to fall on our face when we begin to ponder it.

Let us echo and re-echo, "Let it be done unto me according to your word."

Father Eddie has been on my mind constantly. I can hear his gravelly voice trying to get my attention. Yesterday in my mind's eye, I saw him up in the clouds, with a radiant smile on his face, floating contently down the Madawaska River, high above in the heavens. I often see him like that. Why in that position? Who knows? Probably he is enjoying heaven and simply wants to say hello from time to time. Is this my imagination? Perhaps, but it's fun.

He was trying to say something. It finally came to me. Eddie was a man of contradictions. He struggled with God and got angry. He left the Church because he couldn't have his way. He was a man who knew how to do a good job. In his time he was one of America's top journalists. He was rich. He could grapple with the famous, important, the big shots, and hold his own. He was a big man in the world. He knew how to succeed in terms of earthly values.

Did he sorrow? You bet! He lost two wives—one to influenza and the other to a tragic accident. Finally, as you know, he "sold his soul" for a story, and through that, met his third wife, Catherine. This man began a revolution for all of us.

He followed Catherine through thick and thin, until he was able to marry her, even though it meant sacrificing all his riches for poverty. Eventually he had to give up the marital bed for chastity. And he lived like all of us, in obedience.

This man, who sold all of his words for the Word, became a man of silence, hiddenness and ordinariness. He who was a world traveler, suddenly found himself brought by God into this back bush of Canada, where every human urge that he had previously pursued was slowly being transformed by the mystery of love.

The man of contradictions became a priest of God. Eddie, who was a Roman Catholic rooted in the western mold, became a Melkite priest of that Eastern Rite of the Catholic Church, a contradiction to his natural heritage.

Every facet of Father Eddie's life, from the natural to the supernatural, became a study in contradictions. This man loved women in the human sense of the word. This man loved and was loved by the Mother of God who transformed his human love into a love way beyond anything that the human heart can desire.

Everything he wrote was short, pithy, and profound. He had this incredible gift of taking ordinary earthly things and transforming them with the eyes, the ears, the heart of the gospel. We know that was a grace, because his human gifts did not center around this littleness, humility, ordinariness, and depth of mystery. He knew the gospel language of love both spoken and incarnated.

Today Father Eddie nudged me again; he said, "Go! Discover what I saw when I came the first time to

Combermere." And so I turned to his book, *Hermit Without A Permit:*

"A few days ago, everybody in Madonna House here in Combermere, rushed into my flexible and yielding little desert. The place expanded and became an auditorium and a number of Canadians, men and women staff workers, expressed in prose and poetry, their love and admiration for Canada.

"I was moved and impressed.

"I saw again the railway train that took us, Catherine and I, from Ottawa to Barry's Bay. I saw for the first time, one of the loveliest countries in all the world.

"Our train stopped at many places and stayed there until it made sure it was ready to proceed. At every stop I thought the people were all guests at a party. They looked hearty and more than a little friendly. These people seemed to be my kind of people.

"I had a bad moment when the train stopped at Barry's Bay and I saw the shabby, little wooden depot. It was painted the color of stale chocolate or overdone liver. . . .

"I had come on a visit for two weeks, a vacation. I came from Chicago. I had come reluctantly. I hated the country, or at least thought I did, and I never bothered about my neighbors. I didn't know the names of most of them.

"Life to me at this time was unendurable outside of big cities. I had no intention of staying in Combermere long enough to get hay seeds in my heart.

"I just wanted to see the house that Catherine loved and go swimming in the Madawaska, which she thought was the most beautiful river in the world, and maybe pick some blackberries in the woods.

"So what happened?

"Sitting at the table in the main room in this bleak little house, in the Canadian back bush, I looked out at the majestic river and the tall pines and beautiful maples and the brightness of birch trees. And I said aloud to my own amazement, 'I am going to buy this house and live here.' "[4]

What happened at that moment? That was a moment of the grace of God entering into the heart of this big, wonderful man, who hungered for love and found love in a little house by the Madawaska. He sold, not only all his words for the Word, but he gave up everything that he thought he wanted and took a promise of poverty, chastity and obedience, to become a man of contradiction. An ordinary man who became a priest and who was able to flesh out in his enormous heart and enormous body what happens when a man trusts and takes hold of love himself.

What was his secret? Part of his secret was Our Lady, whom he stayed very close to all of his life. I don't know of anyone who could out-pray him in rosaries. He talked to Our Lady and he was a child of Our Lady and it was she who formed him from the very beginning in this little house, called Madonna House. And out of that, we are able to see what trust in her and trust in her Son, can bring forth for the whole world. The natural life, wedded to the supernatural life, not in extraordinary events, but in ordinary, not in bigness, but in smallness.

Thanks, Father Eddie. Thank you for choosing of your own accord to be a refugee, like your wife, and to show us by leaving your country to come into this beautiful peaceful country, that all of us are on a journey, that we are all homeless until we enter the portals of heaven. It is a short time we have on this earth. It is shot full of glory, because you taught us, and you continue to show us, the presence of God in

4. Eddie Doherty, "First Visit to Combermere." In *A Hermit Without A Permit* (Denville NJ: Dimension Books, 1977), 136.

rocks and flowers and in the natural things of daily life, in food and in one another. You embraced your humanity with gusto and at the same time, held tight to the hand of your heavenly Mother and your Savior. You are teaching us how to walk with joy and with greater love all the time. Thanks for leaving your home and leaving everything for all of us, so that you could be like Abraham, the father of countless, countless souls.

All this leads to following the hidden life the Holy Family lived in Nazareth. What is this life? In the very early pages of the history of the Madonna House Apostolate, Catherine defined her sense of Nazareth:

"To me Nazareth meant, besides the life of poverty, simplicity, peace, and love—the antithesis of the complex Western society that I observed in Toronto and other big cities on the North American continent, and of which I was very tired. A new civilization was being born in the '20s, after World War I, and the rat race we know so well was really beginning to be felt. In these American centers conformity was evident, as were constantly growing materialism and the breakdown of the family. Old traditions were breaking up. There was little peace. Somehow I wanted to get away from all of this, and restore and preserve what was good in the past. I tied it up with my religion in my mind—with the Liturgy, and with the peace of God, purchased through the works of one's hands and not only of one's brains.

"This is what Nazareth meant to me, but it meant more, it meant a novitiate with Our Lord, Our Lady, and St. Joseph . . . a school of love to which I had to go if I were to do what my heart seemingly wanted so much to do, mainly restore the world to Christ."[5]

5. Doherty, *The History of the Apostolate*, Chap. 3.

And so our littleness is obvious and our simplicity is slowly coming into focus and our poverty, personal poverty—being dependent upon God for everything—is growing in the consciousness of all of us. Every little thing is important and nothing should escape our attention as we live every moment of daily life. Bow low before one another. To listen to one another, to have compassion and understanding for the hidden suffering of one another, is imperative at this time. Then we shall rise with Christ on Easter morn as new creations, for the world needs, not mediocre Christians, but saints. Lord Jesus Christ, help us all to be saints.

Acknowledgements

My heartfelt thanks go to Richard Payne for conceiving the idea of this book and for his time and vision in making the selections and bringing them together. Richard's wife Patricia and son Stephen have given invaluable support during the many months of compilation. Their steadfast love, prayer and sacrifice have made this work possible.

I would also like to thank Martin Nagy. Our Lady brought him into this work at the moment it was most needed. His commitment and editorial skills have been an inspiration and a joy.

I would especially thank Rob Huston, who through his love and artistry has given the book its artistic presentation.

Above all I thank Catherine Doherty, Father Eddie Doherty and Father John Callahan for their "*fiat*" to all that the Lord asked of them in bringing forth this vocation.

The priests, laymen and laywomen of Madonna House have received these letters with great love and receptivity to the work of the Holy Spirit in our midst. Each contributed to this work in their own unique way. The concerns of their hearts have often prompted the letters.

I have been working closely for many years with Father Pelton and Albert Osterberger as co-directors of Madonna House, receiving inspiration and encouragement through them. We have grown in love and unity as we move step by step toward sobornost. Daily our hope in Our Lord Jesus Christ is renewed. To them I am deeply grateful.

My greatest gratitude is to Our Lady of Combermere, the heart and soul of Madonna House.

Discover the Marian way to union with Jesus Christ

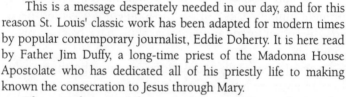

Get right to the very heart of St. Louis de Montfort's 'true devotion' with this new audio presentation!

As St. Louis explains in this classic work, God is everywhere; but nowhere is he closer to us, and more adapted to our humanity, than in the Virgin Mary. It was to make Himself nearer to us that He came to dwell in her. Once we have found Mary, we may find Jesus Christ through her. And through Jesus, we can find the Father.

This is a message desperately needed in our day, and for this reason St. Louis' classic work has been adapted for modern times by popular contemporary journalist, Eddie Doherty. It is here read by Father Jim Duffy, a long-time priest of the Madonna House Apostolate who has dedicated all of his priestly life to making known the consecration to Jesus through Mary.

The complete printed text and consecration cards are also included with this 1 hour abridged audio edition.

1 cassette, 1 hour • $9.95 ($11.95 Cdn) • ISBN 0-921440-57-X

St. Louis de Montfort's True Devotion

The book for all Christians who wish to delve deeper into the Secret of Mary as revealed by St. Louis de Montfort. A best-seller in the Church, it has found its way into the hearts and lives of countless Christians—including Pope John Paul II, who says that "reading this book was to be a turning point in my life... it is an integral part of my interior life and of my spiritual theology."

This modern adaption by Eddie Doherty is in response to a demand for a translation that would take into account contemporary modes of expression.

135 pages • $4.95 ($6.25 Cdn) • Montfort Publications • ISBN 0-910984-02-6

Catherine Doherty's renowned spiritual classic

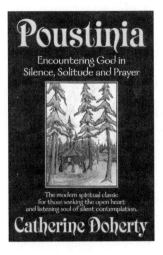

MADONNA HOUSE PUBLICATIONS

COMBERMERE • ONTARIO • CANADA • K0J 1L0

Madonna House Publications is a non-profit apostolate, faithful to the teachings of the Catholic Church.

"Lord, give bread to the hungry and hunger for You to those who have bread," was a favourite prayer of our foundress, Catherine Doherty. At Madonna House Publications, we strive to satisfy both of these fundamental needs.

Through our books, we aim to feed the spiritual hunger for God in our readers with the words of the Gospel and to awaken and deepen in them an experience of Jesus' love in the most simple and ordinary facets of everyday life.

Any proceeds—and donations from friends like you—allow us to assist missionaries with books for people who cannot afford them but most need them, all around the world.

May God bless you for your participation in this apostolate!

To request a catalogue of our current publications, please call (613) 756-3728, or write to us at:

Madonna House Publications
2888 Dafoe Rd
Combermere ON   K0J 1L0
Canada

More information about the Madonna House Apostolate and its publications can be found on the Internet at:

www.madonnahouse.org

Catherine Doherty's cause for canonization as a saint is now in progress. For more information, please visit:

www.catherinedoherty.org